TRUTH in play

TRUTH IN PLAY

Drama Strategies For Building Meaningful Performances

Debbie Nyman and Jill Lloyd-Jones, with David S. Craig

PLAYWRIGHTS CANADA PRESS

Toronto

LIBRARY AND ARCHIVES CANADA CATALOGUING IN PUBLICATION
    Truth in play : drama strategies for building meaningful performances / Debbie Nyman and Jill Lloyd-Jones ; with contributions from David S. Craig.

ISBN 978-1-77091-272-4 (pbk.)

    1. Teenage actors. 2. Theater and youth. 3. Drama--Study and teaching (Secondary). I. Nyman, Debbie, editor II. Lloyd-Jones, Jill, editor III. Craig, David S. (David Stewart), author

PN3160.T44T78 2014   j792.083'5   C2014-904143-8

We acknowledge the financial support of the Canada Council for the Arts, the Ontario Arts Council (OAC), the Ontario Media Development Corporation, and the Government of Canada through the Canada Book Fund for our publishing activities.

Canada Council   Conseil des arts
for the Arts   du Canada

ONTARIO ARTS COUNCIL
CONSEIL DES ARTS DE L'ONTARIO
an Ontario government agency
un organisme du gouvernement de l'Ontario

Canada

Ontario
Ontario Media Development Corporation

CONTENTS

FOREWORD
BY DR. LARRY SWARTZ

A theatre script is a particular kind of text, unique because it demands that the words be lifted from the page; they need to be spoken. A good script speaks to us and about us through voice, gesture, stillness, action. In order to find the meaning of the words, we need to empathize with the character through role-playing and we need to discuss possibilities of speech and action with others. When exploring scripts, we also need guidance from a creative teacher or director who can dip into a palette of strategies to help us bring meaning to the page, to empower us to find meaning, and to work towards strong performances that allow us to convey meanings to an audience. Such beliefs are at the heart of *Truth in Play*.

Jill Lloyd-Jones, Debbie Nyman, and David S. Craig combed through hundreds of published scripts to consider stories and issues that are relevant to twenty-first century learners. Careful consideration has been given to balance gender identities, cultural representations, and social issues drawn from urban and rural experiences from coast to coast. The ten scenes and six monologues were selected to entertain, inform, and stretch our understanding of the world. Students will have opportunities, for example, to sympathize with Anna, who is learning the ins and outs of dating; to struggle with Dane, who is trying to avoid a prison sentence; and to step into the shoes of a Korean Canadian who is trying to convince her immigrant father to support her life choices.

How exciting to have David S. Craig, a professional playwright, help choose scripts of quality and relevance. How exciting to have Debbie Nyman and Jill Lloyd-Jones, who have worked in secondary school settings for over thirty years, offer instructors a menu of drama strategies for students to explore and to work towards deeper understanding of these curated scenes. How exciting to have a source that encourages students to bring life to words written by significant Canadian playwrights in order to find truth in the plays, truth in themselves!

As teachers and students work together inside and outside the scripts in this collection, they will have opportunities to take on the role of performer, director, audience, and playwright. Through the roles they explore, students will move beyond stereotype and enter into the thoughts and feelings of a range of characters. The suggested strategies help students to develop powers of analysis and imagination as they search for meaning in a script and attempt to communicate that meaning to others through presentation or performance. *Truth in Play* will, I am confident, help teachers and students find ways to respect good theatre, respect Canadian theatre, and respect the thrill of breathing life into theatre scripts.

INTRODUCTION

Why This Book?

Miss, where is my script? As experienced drama instructors who love the theatre and all its possibilities, we have heard this question many times. We want to give our students scripts, but only those that speak to them with authentic voices. And once they have such scripts, we want to bring those authentic voices to life with tools and strategies to draw out the meaning of important themes and issues, and to build quality performances to share either in a classroom or in a theatre.

Truth in Play provides students with an abundance of scripts that cover a range of voices, each paired with tools and strategies to guide instructor and student alike into the text and to draw meaningful performances out. These sixteen scenes and monologues are divided into three different sections:

> **Truth in Heart** includes scenes and monologues that explore matters of the heart, such as relationships, trust, identity, teen parenting, and orientation.

> **Truth in Justice** includes scenes and monologues that explore matters of parental and community authority, social justice issues, and generational tensions.

> **Truth in Adversity** includes scenes and monologues that explore the matter of rights and freedoms, both of personal and global significance. Included in this section are two monologues in French, presented in the original language and in English translation.

All of the pieces have been chosen and developed by two experienced authors and curriculum leaders, Debbie Nyman and Jill Lloyd-Jones, with David S. Craig, a professional playwright; director; and actor, adding his perspective in the Notes to the Actors and Directors sections. Bringing the educational voice and perspective together with the playwright and actor's unique skill set has resulted in a rich and multi-layered book for the classroom and theatre.

Who Is This Book For?

This book is designed for instructors to create a shared collective drama experience with both veteran and novice theatre students. But it is also intended as a resource students can use to find a wide variety of contemporary Canadian scenes. The suggested strategies can be used by instructor and student alike to build meaningful interpretations and presentations, allowing students working across curriculums to use this text.

How Do You Use This Book?

Visit any group of students working with scripts and you will see them struggling to find meaning in the text. While compiling this book, we asked ourselves, How can a student come to care about a character with whom they can find no personal connection?, How can they make sense of their cultural experience and identity?, and How can they make an audience care about a world that they themselves don't understand? Students need strategies and techniques to deconstruct, step inside the text, and empathize with what the characters are feeling. This process will lead them to create and share meaningful work. To help achieve this, we have created a set of teaching and learning activities tailored to each piece that we have called Digging Deeper Into the Scene, as well as a map of similar activities designed for the monologues (found on page 179). Accompanying the activities you'll find additional notes for teachers to help guide student learning. The Digging Deeper sections are divided further into four subsections: Exploring Meaning, Building Authentic Characters and Relationships, Rehearsing/Presenting, and Reflecting. Each subsection is meant to invite the student further into the text, building towards more developed understandings and performances.

Exploring Meaning

This section invites students to explore, experiment, and revisit the text to continue to find new meaning in the words. Each time the students engage with the text in a new way they apply a fresh understanding that works towards a multi-layered interpretation of the scene and the characters.

Building Authentic Characters and Relationships

Challenging students to move beyond stereotypes in their portrayal of characters in a scene requires deepened understanding and authenticity. Role-playing from a variety of modes and perspectives will give students a backstory and, in turn, empathy for the characters they are playing.

Rehearsing/Presenting

The exploration and presentation of a scene need not always culminate with a performance. Sometimes rehearsal and presentation can be part of the analyzing, revising, and editing process to work towards a richer performance. We encourage students to share their work in a variety of ways, including those found on page 177. The Notes to the Actors and Directors section that follows Digging Deeper will be helpful to the students as they move towards performance.

Reflecting

Reflection is encouraged throughout the exploration and presentation of the scene. Reflecting in each section informs the work and leads the students to new and deeper understandings of the material. The use of probing questions is designed to trigger thinking, activate creativity and imagination, and stimulate thoughtful, in-depth responses.

In working through Digging Deeper, instructors and students may choose to tackle only one subsection, but attempting all four, layering understanding as you go, will result in the strongest performances. We understand, however, that you may want to use only certain sections and not work through the entire process, or necessarily work towards presentation every time. For these reasons it would make sense to use the Building Authentic Characters and Relationships section if this is the focus of your work, or to only use the Exploring Meaning section if you are concentrating on text and language work. We also encourage instructors to transfer strategies from one scene to another and build their own plan for Digging Deeper.

Preceding every scene, and intended as preparation for Digging Deeper, is Connecting Experience. Best practice amongst educators suggests that students must be given an opportunity to think about and connect with the themes and issues before they embark on the scene. The activities in this section include personal narrative, critical thinking, discussion, and collaboration for students to arrive at a personal and collective understanding of the issues before reading the play text. Activating prior knowledge and experience gives students a meaningful pathway to the scene.

Every scene in the book is also accompanied by a summary of the play in its entirety, background for the scene and characters, further readings and research, and notes to the director and actors. These sections provide practical insights into the scenes and monologues and clues or questions that will help students dig deeper into the material.

Discovering the layers of meaning in a character's dialogue is one of the great joys of the rehearsal process. At the Shaw Festival, actors sometimes spend three weeks doing nothing but analyzing the script so that when blocking begins they are fully aware of all that hidden history, meaning, and feeling that is affecting the character in that moment. Whether working through this book scene by scene or using it to find just one performance piece, we hope that students and instructors take the lessons and strategies learned here into every text exploration, finding the connections that build better understandings and performances. At the very least, we hope that you find the scenes and monologues, all written by contemporary Canadian playwrights, worthy of this attention to find the "Truth in Play."

TRUTH IN HEART

KILT PINS
BY CATHERINE HERNANDEZ

THE PLAY

Kilt Pins is a coming-of-age play that focuses on teenagers attending a Catholic high school in Scarborough, a suburb of Toronto. The central character is Dee, who is attracted to Chris, who is in a relationship with Anna. When Chris begins to notice Dee, Anna reacts by giving Dee a black eye. Chris breaks off his relationship with Anna and pursues a relationship with Dee, which she accepts despite Chris's bad reputation and the misgivings of her friends. This leads to Dee's first sexual experience, which, in turn, leads to intense, complicated feelings and, ultimately, to an unromantic ending. This may sound like a traditional story but the strong emotions of the characters as they navigate adolescence is unique to their time of life and, in slightly different forms, is the subject of drama all over the world.

THE SCENE

The scene takes place at a school dance. Dee's black is almost gone. During her recovery she has been sticking close to her friends and away from Chris, although the attraction on both sides persists. At the dance, Dee, ever responsible, is guarding the punch bowl from being spiked with booze. Chris enters and wants to talk to Dee alone. She refuses and Chris appears to leave but suddenly returns and kisses Dee passionately. The playwright stretches time by allowing Dee to turn to the audience and describe this moment, which then leads to her friends and Chris himself sharing their inner longing.

THE CHARACTERS

Dee: Fifteen years old.
Teresa: Fifteen years old, Dee's friend.
Asha: Fifteen years old, Dee's friend.
Chris: Sixteen years old.
Anna: Fifteen years old.

Imagine there is a handbook to read before you begin dating that is written by young people for young people. Divide into two groups and brainstorm strategies for navigating the dating world.

Choose the five most important points to share with the other group.

SCENE

TERESA begins looking for DEE in the crowd and spots her near the punch bowl.

TERESA: Hey girl. How's the punch?

DEE: Non-alcoholic.

TERESA: Perfect. I knew I could count on you. You can dance, you know.

DEE: It's all right.

TERESA: No, really. You can look over the punch bowl and dance at the same time. I don't mind.

DEE: It's okay.

TERESA: *(indicating DEE's eye)* You can hardly notice, now.

DEE: I know.

TERESA: And she's all the way over there.

DEE: I know.

TERESA: By prom, this'll all be forgotten.

   Pause.

I remember these three bullies. We called them the three Keishas because they were all big, they were all mean, and they were all called Keisha. They gathered all the girls in grade five to stand around me in a circle and made everyone tell me why they didn't like me. So . . .

what I'm trying to say is . . . I don't have a black eye like you, but I know how you feel. And you'll always have us.

ASHA, *out of breath, runs towards the girls.*

ASHA: Oh my God! Oh my God!

TERESA: What?

ASHA: Dee, run to the washroom. Run!

TERESA: What the heck?

ASHA: It's Chris. He just came in.

DEE: Where?

TERESA: Crap! Dee, run!

DEE *tries to push through the crowd.* CHRIS *enters.*

CHRIS: Dee!

TERESA: Jeez! He's coming.

DEE *is still, looking away from* CHRIS *but immovable.*

CHRIS: Dee, could we talk for a minute?

DEE: *(still looking away, stirring the punch bowl)* I have to make sure no one puts alcohol into the punch bowl.

CHRIS: What?!

DEE: I'm . . . You know those Calabra brothers. They're always wanting to . . . do stupid things . . . Like last year's Under the Sea dance. It made a bad name for the dance committee just because of one cup of rum. I don't want anyone to get drunk. I can't take that chance.

CHRIS: Okay.

He begins to walk away.

TERESA: Holy awkward.

ASHA: He's like a stalker or something. Can you believe what just happen—

CHRIS suddenly re-enters and grabs DEE.

TERESA: Holy shit.

They kiss. It is a clumsy kiss through adult eyes, but a movie kiss to teens.

ASHA: Oh my God. They're going to do it.

TERESA: Shut up, Asha!

DEE: This is what it feels like to be kissed. His face comes closer. I can smell him. There's this space between my skin and everyone else around me. But now. But now he comes towards me and breaks the wall. I feel the cold tip of his nose touch mine before he closes the gap completely. I've dreamt of this. Of how our lips will lock. I find his upper lip between both of mine. And I'm burning inside. I'm burning. I hope I'm not shaking. The next thing I know is my eyes are closed. I never want to come up for air. And all I'm thinking is, this is what it's like to be kissed. This is what it's like to be led to the dance floor by a boy. His arms are around my waist, the lights dancing. We fit together. His cheek pressed against my forehead. He runs his fingertips along the back of my bra. I'm shaking. But this is what it's like.

Lights down on the scene, lights up on ANNA, slow dancing, looking downstage.

ANNA: Don't look at them. Look at me. Rule #15: Never look elsewhere. Never look at another girl. Especially while you're dancing with me. A girl walks by with a killer body. But you're with me. So you look at me. This is it, man. Us dancing. You know what's going to happen next, right? The way I'm letting you hold me. The way I'm letting you touch me. You know what's coming next. See this body? It's yours tonight. I knew that would get your attention. We can head over to the Bluffs and listen to music.

Pause.

I'm gonna go to the washroom. I'll meet you at the basketball court.

Lights down on ANNA.

Lights up on ASHA and TERESA, looking longingly at DEE.

TERESA: Rule #11: Never ask a boy to dance.

ASHA: A boy is supposed to ask you.

TERESA: I know I am a budding feminist and all, but I can't. I can't bring myself to ask. I stand here and sway.

ASHA: I stand here, in my new dress. Pretending to listen to Teresa. And I wait.

TERESA: I wait to meet eyes with a guy. But I can only look at my new shoes.

TERESA & ASHA: Maybe next time we'll be just as lucky.

Lights up on CHRIS, slow dancing, looking downstage.

CHRIS: It takes a lot to get here. Are they with another guy? Move on. Are they a loser, standing by the wall? Change directions. Are they special? *(looks at DEE)* Walk forward. Keep walking. Watch to see if they're avoiding eye contact. Do you want to dance? I ask them. Not looking at them. Just a hand extended.

TERESA, ANNA, ASHA & DEE: Sure.

CHRIS: Sure they say. As if they don't care. As if they're not jumping up and down inside. I can feel it. I can feel her shaking when I put my hands around her waist. But sometimes you find a girl. Then you breathe in. Just to smell her.

He approaches DEE.

DEE: What about Anna?

CHRIS: This is where I want to be.

They dance.

Lights up on ANNA. *She's at the basketball court, her party dress still on but with a windbreaker over it. She's smoking and on the phone. Every now and then she spits.*

ANNA: Okay, dude. Listen, just tell Mom I'm with Jessica. Yes, for the night. None of your business. Just tell her. Shut your damn mouth.

She hangs up and dials another number.

Yo. Where are you? I'm here. At the basketball court. Behind the school, you dick. I'm cold. Will you hurry up? Listen. I'm here waiting. You don't keep me waiting. Not when . . . Fine. No. Whatever.

She hangs up. She dials someone else.

Hey. It's me, Anna. I'm at the basketball court. Wanna see me?

DIGGING DEEPER INTO THE SCENE

Exploring Meaning

Text Play

Read the scene silently to yourself.

Form a group of five and read to each other in a circle, but not as the characters. One person begins reading a line and the person beside them reads the next line, etc. Read through in this way twice.

Have each person in the group select a character to read as and read through the scene again. Change characters and repeat.

Change characters again and read the scene standing and facing each other in two lines.

Change again and read through quickly, slowly, loudly, and softly.

Read through the scene while dancing (any kind of dancing).

Notes on Text Play

After reading the scene silently to themselves, you may wish to ask students to sit in a circle reading a line each as a whole class.

Read the scene again in a circle, but begin with a different student.

Form a straight line with your partners across from you and read your lines to each other.

Spread throughout the room and walk towards each other reading your lines.

Choral Speaking

Read through Dee's monologue using three of the strategies for choral speaking found in the Glossary (see page 185).

How could you make this monologue work using all of the female characters speaking together?

Questions

What are five things you know for sure about the scene and characters?

What are five unanswered questions?

Is there anything about the scene you wonder about?

Document your questions and answers, rereading the scene if needed.

Share with a partner, group, or the whole class, noting similarities and differences between the questions.

Which exploration helped you most with your understanding of the scene?

Notes on Choral Speaking

Direct students to the Glossary to choose their own choral-speaking strategy, or work through different strategies together as a class.

Discuss with students how different choral-speaking strategies inform the portrayal of character.

Building Authentic Characters and Relationships

Fact Finding

As individual characters, read through the script and pull out the facts about your character.

Read through again and now add any new thoughts to this list.

In doing this consider:

- Who are you closest to in this scene?
- Who are you afraid of?
- Who do you care about?

Share this information with the group.

Still Image/Tableau

In the first ten lines of the scene we find out that Dee has had a fight. Create a frozen scene (tableau) from the past that gives us some insight into the present conflict.

Bring the scene to life for a moment with minimal movement and using only one word for each character to describe their feelings.

Rehearse and share, ensuring that you have decided what order the words should come in for the most impact.

Create a Working Set

Create a space in the classroom to be your working set.

Consider what you need to create a space that speaks to us about where the characters are, the time of day, etc.

Select music to play in the background to create mood and atmosphere. Think of other things you can do to create a school dance environment.

Notes on Fact Finding

Encourage students to share what they learned about the characters and ask in what ways they can bring the tension of the conflict into their scene.

Notes on Still Image/Tableau

In creating an image of the scene before the event, students will, in an imagined context, have a better understanding of the reasons for the conflict.

Ensure that each group member has a role in the tableau and knows who they are, what side (if any) they are on, and what they may be thinking.

With script in hand, recreate the scene in your working set.

Work through the scene in your set, changing roles each time.

Given what you know right now about *Kilt Pins* and your character, choose one item or prop that your character might have to place on your set.

Find or bring in props and costume pieces that will help you transform your character and the space.

Go to your knapsack or purse to find some items of your own that would work for your character or another character in the group.

Read through the scene again on your set using the necessary props or artifacts.

Work through the scene, following the stage directions carefully and making adjustments for your set.

What blocking problems does the scene present?

How will you solve them?

Creating Atmosphere

Negotiate with your group to select music that can play throughout the scene to enhance or reveal more about the characters and setting.

Experiment and try out various volume levels to match the text levels.

Lighting helps us know whom the focus is on in a scene. Without special lighting, what other techniques will you use to shift the focus?

Notes on Creating a Working Set

In this activity students will begin to have those important discussions about character and context and consider the variety of possibilities connected to both as they recreate the scene and place themselves on the set.

There are challenging blocking questions to solve, dancing, and the monologue in particular. Encourage the students to experiment with a few possibilities and select one that works for them.

Notes on Creating Atmosphere

Assist the students as they attempt to meet the challenges of matching music and focus techniques to the scene.

Encourage them to play with different formations to assist with focus—facing the audience when speaking, facing away from the audience when not; stepping to the centre of the set when speaking, stepping out when not; standing when speaking, seated when not, etc.

Rehearsing/Presenting

Notes on Rehearsing/Presenting

Students might not want to kiss, in which case they may choose another gesture to represent the moment. This can be negotiated amongst the students.

There are a variety of ways to rehearse and present a scene. Many of the above activities and strategies are rehearsal techniques, and at times we use presentation activities during the rehearsal process to further prepare for a performance.

Below is one performance example that you may wish to try for this scene, and you can find even more options by turning to Performance Possibilities on page 177. You can also come up with your own strategies for presenting your scene using these examples as maps. Discuss with your partner or group which presentation strategy works best for your chosen scene.

Join with two other groups working on the scene and together create one working set. Divide the scene into three parts and decide which group will rehearse and present which part. Try to find a natural break in the scene and work out the transitions. How will one group exit the set and the next group come into the set? How will the audience know?

Reflecting

Hot Seat Notes

Encourage the students to ask questions that will deepen their understanding of the characters, questions that will push their thinking beyond their first impression. You may want to have a conversation beforehand to determine which questions would be helpful and brainstorm a list to work from.

You could also put the students interviewing the character in the hot seat in role. They might be guidance counsellors or social workers who have been called into the school to intervene as the conflict is escalating. This will help give the interviewers perspective on the questions they are asking, shifting the burden of the work away from the individual students and giving the questions a framework and purpose.

Hot Seat

Anna is jealous of Dee as she thinks Dee is eyeing "her man" Chris. As a group, work through the Hot Seat strategy from the Glossary (see page 186).

Start with Anna to find out what she thinks is happening, what she has heard, and how she feels about it.

Move on to Dee and, through your questions, find out how she is feeling and what she is going to do with her feelings.

Finally, place Chris in the hot seat. Does he know how Anna and Dee feel? Is there anything he can do to ease the tension and conflict?

Day in the Life

Notes on a Day in the Life

This convention allows students to understand that there may be circumstances that can be misunderstood, or events that can be perceived differently.

A Day In the Life is a drama strategy wherein a day in a character's life is portrayed through a number of scenes. Using this strategy, create the day in three sequences through tableau and limited movement as it really happened for Dee (not as Anna perceived it.)

Share your sequences with the class and discuss what you learned about Dee. Have your feelings about her changed?

Writing in Role

Notes on Writing in Role

Students may choose to write in any of the three roles.

It is important that the writing takes place in silence so that each student may concentrate on what they want to say.

You may wish to play evocative or reflective music or the music selected during the Creating Atmosphere exercise in the background to assist with this process.

In the role of Anna write a letter to Dee sharing your thoughts at the end of the scene. Start with the prompt "I thought that . . . "

In the role of Dee write to Anna, sharing your thoughts. Begin your letter with "I don't understand why . . . "

In the role of Chris, write a letter to Anna or Dee explaining your feelings. Will you apologize? Start with "I want you to know . . . "

Create two or three circles, one inside the other, with those who wrote as Dee in the inside circle and those who wrote as Anna in the outside circle and Chris in the middle.

Read aloud an excerpt from the letter on a signal from the instructor.

Questions

What words resonated for you the most when listening to the voices during the circle share?

How does writing in role help with understanding this scene?

What does Anna know now that she didn't know before?

What do you now know after working with this scene?

Which of the strategies used helped you understand your character the best?

Knowing what you know now, what point might you add to the list you made earlier?

How has this exploration of *Kilt Pins* helped you to consider alternatives to confrontation?

NOTES TO THE ACTORS AND DIRECTORS

In her introduction to the published play, playwright Catherine Hernandez gives this advice: "I need everyone who takes this project on, as a whole or in pieces, to approach all of the characters with the utmost respect. It's very easy for people to resort to caricatures, especially when dealing with teenaged characters. But teens are people who know how to love and feel, and it was in respect for their sexuality and emotions that this play was written." A caricature is a two-dimensional character. "Dumb blond," "babe magnet," "hockey jock," and "computer nerd" are caricatures because they focus the audience on a character with a limited range of feeling and expression. They can be funny but they're not real. Hernandez is serving notice that she sees her characters as three-dimensional. What does that mean for the actors and directors? Hernandez gives a clue in her introduction. The word "respect." Dee, Chris, and Anna are all experiencing powerful feelings. It is your job to enact them respectfully and it is your director's job to help and encourage you to get there. The result will be a very powerful scene.

PLAYWRIGHT AND PRODUCTIONS

Catherine Hernandez is a writer and theatre practitioner who has made an immense contribution to the Toronto theatre scene with her work at Factory Theatre, Native Earth Performing Arts, Theatre Passe Muraille, b current, Carlos Bulosan Theatre, and others. Her first play, *Singkil*, garnered seven Dora Mavor Moore Award nominations, including Best New Play, Independent Division. Catherine is currently Artistic Director of Sulong Theatre Company, which is dedicated to the development of the Filipino Canadian artistic community. *Kilt Pins* was first produced by sulong theatre company and the Kapisanan Philippine Centre for Arts and Culture on December 1, 2011.

READING AND RESEARCHING

Related Resources

On girls and bullying: www.bullyingcanada.ca/content/242548

The meaning of kilt pins at Catholic schools: www.thehairpin.com/2011/08/ex-catholic-schoolgirls-about-that-kilt

An online magazine/blog addressing important issues for teenagers: www.rookiemag.com/

Related Plays

Breakout, edited by Brian Drader (an anthology of five plays by emerging playwrights exploring themes of teen suicide, identity, cultural assimilation, interracial dating, racism, and forgiveness)

In This World by Hannah Moscovitch

Generation NeXXt, edited by Cairn A. Moore (an anthology of scenes exploring adolescent issues for female actors)

Singkil by Catherine Hernandez

OFFENSIVE FOULS
BY JASON LONG

THE PLAY

Christine is mad at Joey. Something happened at the neighbourhood convenience store the night before and it has her wondering if she really knows her boyfriend at all. The owner of the shop, Mr. Chan, is Christine's uncle. Racial insults were yelled at him by some local boys, and Christine has it on good authority that Joey's older brother Doyle was there. Joey denies being there himself, and denies that his brother would be capable of such an act.

The confrontation over this incident forces Joey and Christine to analyze their relationship, their beliefs, their culture, and their identity, and just what being racist means in this day and age. Christine is soon able to peel away the layers of Joey's lies, not only about the incident in Mr. Chan's store, but in the dark truths about how he views her and their differences. The playwright is not content to leave the relationship one-sided. We learn that while Joey has freely admitted he has been dating an Asian girl, Christine has been hiding her relationship to Joey from her parents. In this way, the playwright creates tension between the characters and reveals the subtle, unconscious forms of racism that occur in people who do not think they are racist.

THE SCENE

The scene we have chosen shows Joey being caught in a very serious lie. The stakes are high because if Joey is revealed to be a liar, it could damage his six-month relationship with Christine. The couple is very committed and they are planning a trip to Europe. But to Christine all this is secondary to finding out one thing: who was at Mr. Chan's convenience store last night?

What Joey knows, and Christine doesn't, is that the racial insults directed at Mr. Chan were not made by Joey's brother Doyle, but by Joey himself. This reality fuels Joey's defensiveness and desire to lie. He knows the truth will make him look bad and he doesn't want to lose Christine. What Christine knows, and Joey doesn't, is that Mr.

Chan is Christine's uncle. The family connection fuels her anger and her need to know the truth.

THE CHARACTERS

Christine: Seventeen years old. Chinese.
Joey: Seventeen years old. Caucasian.

CONNECTING WITH THE SCENE

With a partner, discuss what the word "assumptions" means. Do other people make assumptions about you? About the groups you socialize with? Your gender? Your achievements? Where you live? What can you assume about your partner? Are your assumptions close to the truth? How might assumptions affect you, your relationships, and your opportunities for success?

Think of a time in your life when someone else's words hurt you. Did the person saying them understand that you would be hurt? If you didn't speak out then and you could now, what would you want to say? If you are comfortable, share the story with your partner.

SCENE

JOEY enters from stage left. CHRISTINE follows, then stops. JOEY looks back.

JOEY: C'mon. Mac's is this way.

Pause.

CHRISTINE: Let's go to Chan's this time.

JOEY: Why? We never go there.

CHRISTINE: In the mood for change, I guess.

JOEY: But . . . Mac's has way better Slurpees, more selection.

CHRISTINE: It's farther away. I have to be home for dinner soon. Let's just go to Chan's.

JOEY: Actually, you know what? I don't feel like a Slurpee now.

CHRISTINE: You don't?

JOEY: Nah. I had like three Cokes at school today. No more sugar for me.

CHRISTINE: Uh, huh.

>   *Beat.*

You know, you're right. Mac's does have way better Slurpees. Let's go there.

JOEY: You sure?

CHRISTINE: Absolutely. It's worth the extra few blocks. Let's go.

JOEY: Yeah, okay.

CHRISTINE: But I thought you had too much sugar today. Changed your mind twice there in a matter of seconds.

JOEY: I meant I'd go along for the walk; I didn't change my mind.

CHRISTINE: Along for the walk?

JOEY: Yeah.

CHRISTINE: Okay. Walk with me to Chan's then.

JOEY: Fine.

CHRISTINE: Walk with me to Chan's, then when we get there, go inside with me.

>   *CHRISTINE starts off stage right, but JOEY lags behind, stops following. CHRISTINE stops, looks back at him. Beat.*

What would happen, Joe? If you walked into Mr. Chan's store right now? Would he greet you happily? Ask how you've been? . . . Or would he go all quiet? Could he look you in the eye? Would he kick you out, call the cops, would—

JOEY: All right.

CHRISTINE: All right what?

JOEY: I was in the store last night. But I had nothin' to do with—

CHRISTINE: That's two.

JOEY: Two what?

CHRISTINE: That is, at the very least, the second time I've caught you in a big lie this afternoon.

JOEY: It's not that big, I was—

CHRISTINE: I asked you repeatedly, a thousand times, were you in the store last night and you said no.

JOEY: Because I didn't want you to think . . .

CHRISTINE: What? That you're honest?

JOEY: I didn't want you to think badly of me or my brother before you heard all the facts! You weren't there, you don't know what—

CHRISTINE: So tell me.

JOEY: It wasn't as big a deal as—

CHRISTINE: So tell me what happened!

JOEY: Quit interruptin' me and I will!! . . . Mr. Chan shortchanged Doyle. Okay? And he wouldn't admit he messed up . . . Look, I never had a problem with Mr. Chan before but he . . . he was wrong. Doyle just wanted the rest of his change and Chan got all . . . like, defensive. Told us to get out and . . . I mean, Doyle's got a bit of a short fuse but he didn't . . .

CHRISTINE: Struggling to get your facts straight? Or are you just making it up as you go along?

JOEY: Doyle didn't start it, all right?

CHRISTINE: Why should I believe you now?

JOEY: I've never lied to you before.

CHRISTINE: You mean except for those two earlier?

JOEY: "Those two"? Is this some game that I don't know the rules of? You keepin' score?

CHRISTINE: I am not playing around here!

JOEY: Why are you gettin' so worked up about this?

CHRISTINE: Nasty, disgusting words were flung at Mr. Chan last night. Why do you think I'm worked up?

JOEY: I dunno.

CHRISTINE: Mr. Chan is Chinese.

JOEY: Yeah, and?

CHRISTINE: Look at me, Joey. And brace yourself . . . I'm Chinese!

JOEY: I know that.

CHRISTINE: Then how do you think I feel hearing that my boyfriend's brother was hurling racial slurs at a Chinese man?

JOEY: I didn't! And besides, you're not really Chinese.

Pause. CHRISTINE *just stares at him, incredulous.*

I mean, don't take it the wrong way or anything.

Pause. She just stares.

JOEY: See, I think you're taking it the wrong way.

CHRISTINE: How . . . on earth . . . should I take it?

JOEY: You should take it well.

CHRISTINE: I'm not Chinese, you say?

JOEY: Not like Mr. Chan is.

CHRISTINE: Oh my god.

JOEY: What I mean is—

CHRISTINE: No, no. I get it. I don't own a convenience store so I'm not really Chinese, that it?

JOEY: No, I—

CHRISTINE: I don't carry around fortune cookies in my pocket or talk with "wewy wewy tick" accent so I'm not Chinese?

JOEY: I never said that.

CHRISTINE: I didn't spend sixty days in the hull of some oil tanker, smuggled into the country, so I'm not really—

JOEY: Would you let me clarify here? You're blowing this out of . . . You just don't look or act all that, you know . . . ethnic.

> *Pause.*

I'm not sayin' it like it's a bad thing or . . .

> CHRISTINE *just stares at him, stunned.*

What? Why are you looking at me like that?

CHRISTINE: Six months. For six months I said nothing . . . Started small. Little things, but I kept ignoring them.

JOEY: What are you on about now?

CHRISTINE: On our second date we went for dinner at Pappa Pasta and our waiter was Chinese. You asked him for free bread, he said they were out, and after he took our order and walked away you said, "He better not put sweet 'n' sour on my fettuccine."

JOEY: I don't remember that.

CHRISTINE: We were Christmas shopping in that dollar store; you thought the Arabic man behind the counter was "eyeing" you, watching your every move, so on your way out you make some muttered dig about how he should never be allowed on an airplane.

JOEY: Come on, Chris, that was a joke. It had nothing–

CHRISTINE: "East Indians are cheap." "Duck down! That Asian gang's packin' heat!" "Why you grow so small? Rice overdose?"

JOEY: Oh gimme a break. Are you–

CHRISTINE: It never, NEVER occurred to you that any of that stuff might be hurtful to me?

JOEY: It had nothin' to do with you.

CHRISTINE: Because I'm not really "ethnic."

JOEY: No, I don't think of you like that. I think of you as a girl, a girl I like, that's it.

Jeez, Chris, they were just jokes. Words.

CHRISTINE: So words can't hurt? Jokes can't hurt?

Exploring Meaning

Text Play

Read the scene silently to yourself.

Read the scene out loud by yourself.

Read the scene out loud with a partner.

Change roles and read it out loud again.

Read the scene out loud to each other while sitting back to back.

Read the lines together while doing a variety of activities, such as exercising, doing homework, playing catch, etc.

Read the scene to each other while walking through the space, imagining, as in the scene, that you are walking down the street. What would you notice on the street? How will the audience know you are walking outside?

Questions

What five things do you know for sure about the scene and characters?

What five unanswered questions do you have?

What do you wonder about?

Document your responses, rereading the scene if needed.

Share with a partner, group, or the whole class, noting similarities and differences between the questions.

Notes on Text Play

Choose a variety of ways to unpack the text of the scene so that students have opportunities to explore it. Encourage the students to continue switching parts to become familiar with both characters. Only after significant exploration invite the students to make their choice of which character to play.

Building Authentic Characters and Relationships

Role On the Wall

Create an outline of a girl and a boy using large sheets of paper and post them at the front of the room.

Using a coloured marker, record everything you know for sure about Christine and Joey outside of their outline. For example, they're students, they've been going out for six months, etc.

With a different colour of marker, write down everything you know about their relationship in the space between the characters.

With yet another colour, write down everything you think you know about them inside their outlines—their feelings, their fears, their hopes, etc.

Finally, in a fourth colour and on the edges of the paper, write down all of the assumptions and perceptions people in their lives make about Joey and Christine. For example, how would their teacher describe them? Their friends? Their parents?

Face to Face

Return to the script with this new understanding of Christine and Joey. Sit and face your partner, making eye contact. Look down on the page, find your line, look up and make eye contact again, and say the line. Continue through the script in this way. You must make eye contact with each line! After going through the script once in this way, discuss with your partner the places where it felt right to be looking directly at your partner. Were there moments in the script where it felt awkward and out of character to be looking at each other?

Read the lines, trying to make eye contact when you are speaking and avoiding eye contact when your partner is speaking. Are there moments where this feels right?

Share these observations with your partner.

Notes on Finding the Essence

Students can share these words with their partners or bring two or three pairs together to share the words. It will be interesting for them to notice if others chose similar words. This activity will encourage thoughtful character analysis.

Notes on Creating a Working Set

A possible challenge for the students in this scene will be walking and moving while playing the scene, interacting within the space to create the illusion they are on their way to Chan's. Encourage the students to be natural and authentic.

What Are They Thinking? Notes

Students can respond individually in their scenes by "thinking out loud," or all groups can freeze and individuals could be prompted to speak their thoughts in the presence of the whole group.

The monologues could be further developed into "stand-alone" pieces to be analyzed and presented.

Finding the Essence

Read the text again, reducing each line to what you feel is the most important word. Read these lines with your partner, only saying the word you've chosen, but communicate the meaning with gestures.

Share with the whole class three strong words from the exercise that best describe your character's feelings. Explain why you chose these words.

Create a Working Set

How will you create the outside world? Are Christine and Joey in a public place? Are they walking to a destination? Find or bring in props and costume pieces that will help you transform the space.

Read through the scene again on the set with the necessary props.

What Are They Thinking?

Play the scene again from the beginning. On a signal, you will be asked to freeze at different points in the script and to "think out loud" for a moment. This will help you learn more about what your character and your partner's character might be thinking or feeling in that moment. Stay in role as you share your thoughts. You may wish to start with "What I really hope is . . . " "What I want is . . . " or "What I am afraid of is . . . "

Following the exercise choose one of the prompts and develop a short monologue that will help you better understand your feelings in role.

Sit back to back with your partner and share your monologues.

Discuss with your partner what you learned about the characters and, most importantly, about their relationship that you can now include in the scene.

Rehearsing/Presenting

There are a variety of ways to rehearse and present a scene. Many of the above activities and strategies are rehearsal techniques, and at times we use presentation activities during the rehearsal process to further prepare for a performance.

Below is one performance example that you may wish to try for this scene, and you can find even more options by turning to Performance Possibilities on page 177. You can also come up with your own strategies for presenting your scene using these examples as maps. Discuss with your partner or group which presentation strategy works best for your chosen scene.

Join with another pair of students and divide the scene into two parts so that each pair will present one half of the scene. A natural break in the script where you might change actors is at Christine's line, "I'm not fooling around here." To make the transition as smooth as possible, the actors can hold their positions after that line, the two new actors enter the scene, take their exact positions and props, maybe even a costume piece from the actors, and continue the scene while the previous actors leave the set. Christine could repeat her line and continue the scene. Practise the transition before presenting the scene.

Reflecting

If I Were You . . .

Notes on If I Were You . . .

This activity will encourage the students to address their own opinions and thoughts with an opportunity to further discuss the issues presented in the scene.

Following the presentations, two students volunteer to play the roles of Christine and Joey and freeze in their final position in the scene. Consider advice you might give to the characters. Do words hurt? Is Joey racist? What would you do if you were in this relationship?

One at a time, approach one of the characters and choose to make a physical connection or not, and complete the line, "If I were you . . . "

Allow the students time after they have completed the journal entry to highlight or choose the most important excerpt of the piece. Ideally, the excerpt would give the listener an idea of the choices the characters made after the scene, of how they might have changed. It can be effective to move from a Christine reading to a Joey reading and to sometimes return to a student. Remind them to be prepared to read more than once.

Discuss the variety of responses following the reading.

Writing in Role

Write a journal entry in the role of either Christine or Joey two years later, following high school. Describe what you are doing now. Did you go to university? Did you stay together? Did you rebuild trust in each other or did you end the relationship? How do you feel about it now?

Create two circles, one inside the other, with those who wrote as Joey in the inside circle and those who wrote as Christine in the outside circle.

Read aloud an excerpt from your journal on a signal from the instructor.

NOTES TO THE ACTORS AND DIRECTORS

The scene begins casually, with both characters hiding their intentions. The scene builds in intensity as Christine catches Joey in one lie after the other. Mark these places in the script and decide how these discoveries affect each character. There is a build (sometimes called "a rising tension") towards the reveal, which is that Joey doesn't think of Christine as being Chinese (refer to the "What Are They Thinking?" activity to develop this aspect of the scene).

The playwright gives the actors valuable information about the pacing of the scene through his use of punctuation. Notice how many of Joey's lines end with a dash ("–"). This indicates that Christine is interrupting Joey. The execution of an interruption requires split-second timing, so it's good practice for the actor playing Joey to have one or two extra words after the interruption so he can really feel cut off. Write those words in your script. As well as the dash, notice how often the playwright uses an ellipsis (" . . . "). How does that punctuation affect the way you say the line?

Joey's defensiveness around his wrongdoing is classic. He tries to hide it, but once he is caught he tries to minimize it. "They were just jokes," he says. The scene will have a stronger impact if the actor playing Joey really believes this is true so we, the audience, can see it is not.

PLAYWRIGHT AND PRODUCTIONS

Jason Long is a playwright and screenwriter from Calgary, Alberta, and a graduate of the National Theatre School's Playwriting Program. Jason continues to write screenplays and to work on projects for Quest Theatre in Calgary. *Offensive Fouls* has toured extensively across Canada, with productions from several theatre companies. Of the play, Jason wishes to remind us that "*Offensive Fouls* unfolds in real time. If properly executed it does not give the audience a moment to breathe, or check in with themselves or deconstruct what they have just witnessed!"

READING AND RESEARCHING

Related Resources

A review of the book "*Too Asian?*" an anthology of essays that explore racism in Canada's universities and how the media illustrates that dialogue: www.rabble.ca/books/reviews/2012/09/too-asian

Information about Debwewin's Canadian Anti-Racism Community initiative: www.debwewin.ca/antiracismcommunity.htm

The homepage for FAST, Fighting Anti-Semitism Together, which includes information about to help fight racism, sexism, and other concerns surrounding inequality: www.fightingantisemitism.com/

CKNW Vancouver's coverage of the Canadian federal government's apology to Chinese Canadians for years of legislated racism, particularly surrounding the Chinese Head Tax: www.cknw.com/2014/05/14/35637/

Related Plays

Banana Boys by Leon Aureus

Mother Tongue Betty Quan

Love and RelASIANships, volumes 1 and 2 by Nina Lee Aquino (anthologies of contemporary Asian Canadian drama)

Mom, Dad, I'm Living With A White Girl by Marty Chan

paper SERIES by David Yee

Generation NeXXt, edited by Cairn A. Moore (an anthology of scenes concerning adolescent issues for female actors)

AGOKWE
BY WAAWAATE FOBISTER

THE PLAY

Waawaate Fobister wrote this award-winning one-man play when he was in his early twenties. It is based on his experiences growing up as a gay youth on a small First Nations reserve north of Kenora, Ontario. He has spoken in interviews of having a stable home life despite living in a community dealing with serious problems like poverty, mercury poisoning, alcoholism, diabetes, high unemployment, forced relocation, and suicidal youth. He was the first member of his family tree to graduate from high school. It was not a supportive place for anyone who was different, let alone someone who was gay.

In the play, originally performed solo by Fobister himself, the actor portrays the central character, Jake, and a host of other minor and major characters, including the narrator, Nanabush, the Ojibwe shape-shifting trickster.

THE SCENE

The scene we have chosen from *Agokwe** begins with Nanabush commenting on Jake and his struggle to accept his homosexuality. We then see Jake meeting Mike, a boy he has been attracted to and believes is attracted to him. Can he reveal himself? The stakes are high. If he has guessed wrong, it could be more than just humiliation. It could mean being ostracized, perhaps violently, by his community. What they discover first is a mutual admiration around movement. Mike admires Jake's dancing and Jake admires Mike's skating. Then they reveal their inner selves. This acceptance, and the relief from uncertainty and fear, is the climax of the scene.

Although this scene—and the entire play—was impressively performed by one actor, we can imagine it being staged by three. While the characters of Jake and Mike are obviously male, it would be interesting to perform the scene with a male cast and then with a female cast to see what differences this choice creates.

---

* Pronounced ah-GOO-kway.

THE CHARACTERS

Nanabush: A spirit, a teacher, a trickster. (Traditionally male but could be played by any gender.)
Jake: A teenager and traditional Ojibwe Grass dancer.
Mike: A teenager and hockey player.

CONNECTING WITH THE SCENE

How do you know if someone is attracted to you? What are some of the signs that can be communicated to you indirectly? Even if you feel the same way towards another person, what might stop you from acting upon or sharing your feelings? Share your thoughts and stories on this topic with a partner.

Think about who, as a society, we discriminate against, then as a collective create a list of the groups or people you came up with. Work in a small group and share with each other a time when you discriminated against someone, or witnessed such discrimination. How might we change this from continuing to occur in society?

SCENE

NANABUSH: Jakey? Jakey? Where did li'l Jakey go? Oh, there he is. Awww . . . crying like a little girl because his weenug let him down. Wandering all alone in the dark like so many of my lost people because they cannot see the light that shines within them. The light that can only shine bright when one is true to oneself. Agokwe, Jakey, Agokwe. It's okay to cry. It takes great strength to cry like a woman, but cry for the right reasons. Self-pity is a waste of time. Come on, girl, man the fuck up. Not one spirit but two, that is the light that shines within you. There is a fire that burns in your heart like another who wanders alone in the dark. The fire will guide you on the wings of a dove. Go to the fire and find your true love.

The sounds of branches breaking.

MIKE: Hello, is someone there?

JAKE: Sorry. Am I intruding? I was walking in the woods and I saw the fire. Do you want to be alone?

MIKE: Doesn't make any difference to me. Don't I know you?

JAKE: Huh? No, we've never met.

MIKE: You look familiar. I've seen you somewhere before.

JAKE: Maybe at the party.

MIKE: No, not the party, somewhere else, maybe at a powwow? You're a Grass dancer, right?

JAKE: Yeah, that's right.

MIKE: Your colours are blue, white, and red. Your head roach is pretty cool too.

JAKE: Wow. You remember my colours?

MIKE: I remember your white eagle feathers because they are so rare. I also remember seeing you dance. You weren't like any of the other dancers. You had your own style. You were like the grass blowing in the wind. You looked so free, like you didn't have a care in the world.

JAKE: That's how I feel when I'm dancing.

   Beat.

But I always have these intense butterflies floating around in my stomach and I feel like I'm going to puke.

MIKE: That's exactly how I feel every time I am about to play a game. I get those nasty butterflies too.

JAKE: Huh. I would've never guessed because you seem so brave on the ice. By the way, my name is Jake.

MIKE: Mike.

JAKE: Yeah, I know who you are. Everyone knows who you are.

MIKE: They think they know me but they have no idea.

JAKE: I think I know what you mean.

MIKE: You do?

JAKE: Do you go to the Kenora Shoppers Mall often?

> *Beat.*

I think you know what I'm talking about. I saw you. You saw me. And I think we both know who we really are.

MIKE: What the hell are you talking about?

JAKE: I . . . I'm . . . I think we play on the same team. And I'm not talking about hockey.

MIKE: Are you a fag?

JAKE: I don't know what I am but I know you were staring at me at the mall, and I was staring at you. I think we both know what was going on.

> *Beat.*

And if you want to beat the shit out of me right now, go ahead. But I have to tell you, I like you. I don't know why. I don't know how, but I do. I like you. So go ahead, beat the shit out of me; it wouldn't be the first time.

> *MIKE laughs.*

MIKE: And you think I'm the brave one?

> *JAKE and MIKE kiss.*

NANABUSH: Not one spirit but two, that is the light that shines within both of you. In this world twin flames can meet in the dark. When they come together they ignite true love's spark.

JAKE: I can't believe this is finally happening . . . feels good . . . scary.

> *He looks at MIKE, who is crying.*

What's wrong? Why are you crying?

MIKE: Fuck! Because I'm scared too. I've been fighting this for so long. Pretending to be somebody–this fake somebody–but too scared to be a real nobody. The first time I really noticed you was at the powwow. I had no idea who you were, but when I saw you I thought you were so beautiful in your regalia and I was confused and pissed off because you made me want something I knew I shouldn't want. But when I saw you dancing I couldn't take my eyes off you, no matter how pissed off I was. After the powwow I tried to put it out of my head, but when I saw you at the Kenora Mall all of those feelings came back and I wanted to punch you in the face to make it stop. But instead I couldn't stop myself from staring at you, and when you looked back I chickened out and took off.

JAKE: There's no reason for us to be scared anymore.

JAKE and MIKE kiss again.

DIGGING DEEPER INTO THE SCENE

Exploring Meaning

Text Play

Read the scene silently to yourself.

Read the scene out loud by yourself.

Read the scene out loud with a partner.

Change roles and read it out loud again.

Change partners and read the scene together.

Change roles and read it again.

Read the scene whispering to each other, then read it loudly to each other.

Read the scene walking around and then standing and facing each other.

Notes on Text Play

Choose a variety of ways to unpack the text of the scene so that students have opportunities to explore it. Ensure that the scene is explored in many ways, with the students changing roles each time, exploring different gender pairings as this can often change the interpretation of the scene.

Questions

What five things do you know for sure about the scene and characters? Create a character profile of your role based on the information in the scene.

What five unanswered questions do you have about the character or scene? What do you wonder about? Document your questions, rereading the scene again if needed.

Share your questions with a partner, group, or the whole class, noting similarities and differences between each query.

Building Authentic Characters and Relationships

Finding the Truth in the Character

Notes on Finding the Truth in the Character

Students may find props in the room or in their personal effects or even bring them into class. You may want to model the activity in role for the students.

This may also lead to a discussion of props and costume choices.

Consider and find two props that are important to your character that could be used throughout the scene. The prop might be something that is kept hidden from the audience and your partner but tells us more about your character.

Share these props with your partner before you begin the scene to reveal information about the character. Describe the props in role. For example, "This is a knife my grandfather gave me that I carry because I am afraid of . . . "

You may question your partner further to learn more. Have they ever felt the need to use it? Where do they carry it?

Try to use at least one of the props as you play the scene.

Finding the Truth in the Relationship

Notes on Finding the Truth in the Relationship

Encourage the students to work hard to make and even hold eye contact in the exercise. Discuss with the students how people in society sometimes avoid eye contact and why.

Play the scene through trying not to make eye contact with your partner by either turning your head, moving away, etc.

Play the scene again, this time trying to make eye contact on every line.

When did it make sense to avoid eye contact and when did it feel right to make eye contact? Why is it difficult to make eye contact? How can you communicate this to the audience? Discuss these questions with your partner.

Play the scene incorporating some of these choices.

The Kiss

Notes on The Kiss

Some students may not be comfortable with the kiss. Exploring alternatives will help them find a gesture that will communicate the feelings comfortably. This could lead to an important discussion about any physical contact on stage.

Consider with your partner three ways that you could show the feeling and power of the moment of the kiss, without actually kissing. Even if you and your partner are comfortable with the kiss, consider if the audience would be comfortable or if they would respond negatively and miss the impact of the moment.

Experiment with the options and choose the most effective alternative.

Create a Working Set

Notes on Creating a Working Set

Encourage the students' creativity when transforming the room into an outdoor setting. Ask students to imagine different types of wooded areas and what each might contain and look like.

Create a working set for the scene. How will you establish the outside world with minimal lighting and set pieces? How will we know from the way the characters move that we are in an outside place?

Rehearse the scene in the set with the props from the previous activity.

Rehearsing/Presenting

There are a variety of ways to rehearse and present a scene. Many of the above activities and strategies are rehearsal techniques, and at times we use presentation activities during the rehearsal process to further prepare for a performance.

Below is one performance example that you may wish to try for this scene, and you can find even more options by turning to Performance Possibilities on page 177. You can also come up with your own strategies for presenting your scene using these examples as maps. Discuss with your partner or group which presentation strategy works best for your chosen scene.

This scene is brief and we suggest that you rehearse and play the entire scene as it is written. You may want to record Nanabush's lines to play back during the performance, or you may wish to ask another student to read this part. Will the characters be on stage when Nanabush is speaking? Will they enter during or after the speech?

Reflecting

Corridor of Voices Notes

Ask for a volunteer (male or female) to take on the role of Jake and listen to the voices as they walk down the corridor. As an option, the facilitator may take on this role. To ensure each person speaks, make eye contact or nod to indicate whose turn it is.

If the students are having difficulty with their advice, prompt them with "I think you should because . . . "

The activity should be played out quietly, with everyone listening to the advice of the others.

Ask the volunteer to share how they felt moving through the corridor.

Corridor of Voices

What would friends and family say? Take on the role of either Nanabush or one of Jake or Mike's friends or elders (be sure you know who you are). In the role, give advice to Jake about what to do next. Should he stay in Kenora or go away to the big city where it may be easier to become invisible.

As a group form two lines face to face, making a four-foot-wide corridor. Choose one person to play the role of Jake, who will walk slowly down the corridor listening carefully as each person in turn from one line to the other gives him or her advice.

At the end of the corridor Jake will turn and say what he has decided to do based on the advice, stating his reasons.

Collective Poem

In a group, think about the possible consequences of the choices that Jake and Mike have made. What are they risking?

Discuss what can be done about discrimination when it happens. What are the risks of taking action?

Why is it important to stand up for someone even when the group is against you?

As a group, create a poem that represents your feelings and is a positive message for anyone in that situation. Order each pair of lines so that the poem builds to the final two.

Encourage students to consider not only the meaning of the words in their poems, but also how they will theatrically present them in the space by using specific formations to enhance their work. They could stand in a straight line, walk on one by one, form a semicircle, or start with their backs to the audience, each turning around to read their line.

Arrange another group to listen to the poems and give positive feedback.

Groups can share one by one or half the group can share as the rest listen.

You may create your own eleven-line poem or use the prompts:

Hold on!
Hold on to . . .
Even if . . .
Hold on to . . .
Even if . . .
Hold on to . . .
Even if . . .
Hold on to . . .
Even if . . .
Hold on to . . .
Even when . . .

Work carefully to negotiate choices around words and meanings to create a powerful statement for those who have the courage to be themselves.

Create a title for your poem.

Performance Poetry

Think about the meaning of the words.

As a group, rehearse your work using a number of choral strategies.

Mark down the group's decisions about how your poem will be performed verbally to create the maximum impact and then rehearse.

Once everyone is confident with the verbal part of the performance, start to work on the use of space and formations, gesture, and physicality to add more meaning to the poem.

Rehearse and share your work with another group, asking for positive feedback and suggestions for changes.

Incorporate any suggestions that will further develop your work.

NOTES TO THE ACTORS AND DIRECTORS

Nanabush begins the scene in a mocking tone. But he is not mocking Jake's tears, only his self-pity. The act of crying he honours. "It takes great strength to cry like a woman." This is part of the power that the playwright sees in Agokwe—two-spirited, men and women. Consider how that sentiment would play out in a small community or even in a city high school. Is it brave? Revolutionary? Social suicide?

The scene is simple but powerful. Jake takes a huge risk and reveals his attraction. What gives him this courage? There is Nanabush's encouragement, of course, but what is it that Mike says that gives Jake the courage to be so honest?

The script says "Jake and Mike kiss." How was this performed by one actor!? For two actors, in an academic setting, it would be an incredibly powerful moment, but it would also be challenging for some people in the audience. Discuss how you imagine your audience will respond. Will it be positive or could it push some people into a negative reaction? If a kiss seems inappropriate, what could replace it that would still represent an intimate moment?

This is a deeply personal scene. The characters are vulnerable and the actors should be too! Exploring the above activity, "Finding the Truth in the Relationship," will allow you to experience and communicate these feelings authentically.

PLAYWRIGHT AND PRODUCTIONS

Waawaate Fobister was born on the Grassy Narrows First Nations Reserve near Kenora in Northern Ontario. Says Fobister about his heritage, "The Anishinaabe people were always storytellers. It's been a huge part of our culture, and theatre, to me, is the modern way of storytelling." *Agokwe* premiered at Buddies in Bad Times Theatre, Toronto, in their 2008/2009 season. The play went on to win six Dora Mavor Moore Awards and has toured nationally.

Related Resources

These clips are examples of performance poetry and authentic representations of persevering through discrimination against gay people. Review any clips you may wish to show, keeping the maturity and suitability for your group in consideration. The YouTube resources contain mature content and strong language.

Dear Straight People performed by Denice Frohman:
www.youtube.com/watch?v=5frn8TAlew0

Fat Girl performed by Megan Falley:
www.youtube.com/watch?v=vxgpCfPqQpk

That Line Was So Gay: www.youtube.com/watch?v=XVVMr4f9Cto

Love Is All You Need?: www.youtube.com/watch?v=CnOJgDW0gPl

The official Tomson Highway website:
www.tomsonhighway.com/biography.html

Related Plays

The Gay Heritage Project by Damien Atkins, Paul Dunn, and Andrew Kushnir

Perfectly Abnormal: Seven Gay Plays by Sky Gilbert

Outspoken: A Canadian Collection of Lesbian Scenes and Monologues, edited by Susan G. Cole

Harriet's House by Tara Goldstein

The Other Side of the Closet by Ed Roy

The Rez Sisters by Tomson Highway

Bannock Republic by Kenneth T. Williams

MOSS PARK
BY GEORGE F. WALKER

THE PLAY

Moss Park is the story of Tina and Bobby, two young people with few options and a hard decision in front of them. Tina is raising their daughter, Holly, by herself because Bobby can't seem to hold down a job. He wants to be responsible. He really does. He just keeps having trouble with stuff, like making decisions. When Tina gets pregnant again, the prospect of having two infants freaks her out so she's considering ending the pregnancy. What she needs from Bobby is something solid, something real. She's even willing to consider Bobby becoming a professional thief if it means she can provide for her child. She'll do anything to avoid making that hard decision.

THE SCENE

Tina needs help and she's really hoping Bobby can provide it. Realistically he can't, but where else can she go? Rock and a hard place. Bobby wants Tina to love him the way he loves her, the way people love each other in the movies. But she keeps asking him for things he doesn't have, like a place to live. She keeps hoping he'll come through, but if he doesn't she will take matters into her own hands. Because soon she will be homeless, which means a shelter, and how can she survive that with two kids? She can't. She won't.

THE CHARACTERS

Tina: Twenty years old.
Bobby: Twenty years old.

Imagine that you are a single parent of a two-year-old child. You require financial assistance and receive $1600 each month from government programs. You are looking for a job but you will have to earn enough money to also pay for daycare. Working with a partner or in a small group, create a budget for how you would use the money. Your budget must include housing, food, expenses for your child (clothes, medication, etc.), and personal expenses. Do not leave anything out! Share your budget with another group. Were there similarities and differences? What did you find most challenging about this exercise? Apart from budgeting your money, consider other challenges a single parent would face.

When is love not enough? Think of a situation where the fact that you love someone is not enough to be in a relationship. Have you ever felt this way? How did you proceed? Share your thoughts with a partner.

SCENE

TINA: Yeah. I guess it is. Look, have you got any money?

BOBBY: On me?

TINA: On you, in the bank, under your mattress, wherever.

BOBBY: There's a cheque. The carpet store owner owes me for a day's work. But it needs to be picked up.

TINA: Okay so could you do that? I need to buy some things for Holly.

BOBBY: Like what?

TINA: Do you really need to know? Can't you just get the cheque like I asked?

BOBBY: No.

TINA: Why not, Bobby?

BOBBY: Well it's just that I'm a little scared of the guy. I think he came pretty close to hitting me when he found out about the van's transmission.

TINA: So you'll just have to suck it up, won't you. I need money. Holly needs new shoes.

BOBBY: Already? What's wrong with the ones we just bought her?

TINA: You mean three months ago?

BOBBY: She needs a new pair after just three—

TINA: They don't fit.

BOBBY: Are you sure?

TINA: She says they hurt her. Maybe she's lying. Maybe you should just come over and shake the truth out of her. Find out what the hell the little bitch is trying to pull.

BOBBY: Come on, Tina, I was just—

TINA: They don't fit! Okay!?

BOBBY: Sure. Yeah . . . And your government allowance didn't come?

TINA: It came and went. You have to go get that cheque.

BOBBY: It's not much.

TINA: It's better than nothing.

BOBBY: He might want to hold on to it to cover the expense of getting the transmission fixed.

TINA: He can't do that. It's against the law.

BOBBY: Are you sure?

TINA: No. But it's what you could tell him.

BOBBY: Could you?

TINA: What?

BOBBY: You could take Holly. I mean even if he doesn't care what the law is, if you're standing there with a toddler looking really sad or maybe even crying . . . that's gotta make him wanna hand it over.

TINA: Jesus! You want me to cry. Are you sure you don't want me to beg too? Hey maybe I could dress Holly in rags and wipe shit on her face.

BOBBY: Come on. It was just a sugges–

TINA: You have to start getting it together, Bobby! You really do!!

BOBBY: Like you think I don't know that. There's nothing I want more in the freakin' world than to get it together!

(touches her hair) You know, so you'll let me be with you and our child.

> *He kisses her. They hug. Then suddenly she pushes him away.*

TINA: No.

BOBBY: No what?

TINA: This isn't that movie.

BOBBY: What?

TINA: It's not that movie or that TV show or whatever it is you've got in your head. It's our life. And it's still fucked up and some kiss isn't going to . . . Look whatever you have to do, just do it for yourself, okay. Don't go thinking about me and you and Holly in that way. I mean all together.

BOBBY: Why not?

TINA: Because it might not happen.

BOBBY: It has to happen. That's the way it's supposed to be.

TINA: In your movie . . .

BOBBY: No, for real. It's gotta happen for real.

TINA: Maybe. But it's too hard. Trying to make it happen is just too hard. And scary . . . and sad. I can't rely on you.

BOBBY: I know that. Not right now you can't. But this is just a phase I'm going through.

TINA: No it's not. Unless you've been in this "phase" since we met, when you were just turning nine.

BOBBY: That wasn't a phase. That was just me. You know, and my problems with . . .

TINA: Concentrating.

BOBBY: Yeah or . . .

TINA: Making decisions.

BOBBY: Yeah all that stuff. That's just me. This is an actual phase where I can't hold on to a job and earn money on a regular basis. I've earned money in the past though, right. I had a job I didn't get fired from. It's not my fault that factory closed. I was really thrown by that, you know. I thought I had a job for life. Okay, it wasn't anything I really wanted to do, but I was willing to hang in there basically forever. So I got thrown. And it's like I've got . . . you know, post-traumatic stress. It really is.

> *A vehicle passes with its siren blaring. BOBBY watches it until it is out of sight. TINA watches BOBBY then just puts her head down.*

(turning back to her) Why you doing that, T? Why do you have your head between your legs like that? You crying?

TINA: No . . .

BOBBY: You are, aren't you. You're crying.

TINA: I'm not crying, Bobby.

(lifting her head) I was just thinking.

BOBBY: Thinking about what?

TINA: Us. What else?

BOBBY: What about us.

TINA: Everything about us.

BOBBY: Does everything include if you still love me? Was that part of what you were thinking?

TINA: No.

BOBBY: So you do then? You still love me?

(sits next to her) Because I still love you a lot.

 She is just looking at him.

TINA: So what?

BOBBY: Whaddya mean so what?

TINA: I mean I've got problems right now way bigger than who loves who. Or who doesn't. My mom and I are getting evicted.

DIGGING DEEPER INTO THE SCENE

Exploring Meaning

Text Play

Read the scene silently to yourself.

Then read the scene silently with a partner.

Read the scene out loud facing your partner.

Choose a variety of ways to unpack the text of the scene so that students have opportunities to explore it. Encourage the students to continue to switch parts to become familiar with both characters. Only after significant exploration invite the students to make a choice of which character to play.

Discuss how the exercises informed their roles, the setting, and the action of the scene. When did it feel authentic? When did it feel right for the scene?

Change roles and read it again sitting side by side. How did it feel different? Which position felt "more real"?

Change roles and read it out loud again.

Read the scene sitting back to back, imagining that you are speaking to each other on cellphones.

Read the scene moving as though you were in a park. Imagine you are in a playground.

Read the scene with one character angry and the other calm throughout. Change emotions and read through again.

Read the scene sitting or standing very close to each other and then a distance away.

Questions

What five things do you know for sure about the scene and characters?

What five unanswered questions do you have? What do you wonder about?

Document your responses, rereading the scene if needed.

Share with a partner, group, or the whole class, noting similarities and differences between the questions.

Notes on Questions

Discuss with the students the difference between "what we know for sure" in a scene and "what we think we know or assume."

Building Authentic Characters and Relationships

What Do I Want? Objectives and Motivation

Meet with the other students playing your character, one group for Tina and one group for Bobby, and separately identify issues and challenges facing your character.

Students can work in
groups of four or five to
discuss the characters
and create the theatre
pieces.

Working in groups
of the same charac-
ter encourages the
students to deepen
their understanding of
the character as they
share their different
interpretations.

Discuss and share your ideas of what your character wants most in this scene and in the future. Begin the discussion by sharing your favourite line in the scene—the line you like reading or saying and feel represents the essence of the character. Justify your choice to the group.

Decide together what your character wants in the scene and write it out in the first person. For example, "I want . . . "

How could the character most effectively communicate what she/he wants and needs?

Select two or three lines from the scene. Create a theatre piece using these words, integrating voice, tableau, movement, and gesture to communicate what your characters want in this scene and in their future, either together or apart.

What did you learn about Bobby in the presentation?

What did you learn about Tina?

How will you bring these new understandings into your scene?

Return to the scene and integrate this new understanding.

Improvisation

Improvising allows the
students to become a
character more fully as
they express the char-
acter's thoughts and
feelings in their own
words. This also allows
the students to step out
of their roles as Bobby
and Tina and listen as
a friend or confidante.
They will develop
empathy for the char-
acter as they listen and
improvise.

Consider whom Tina and Bobby might turn to for support and advice.

Students playing Bobby in the scene will take on the role of the person Tina would turn to for advice.

Imagine that Tina is meeting with this person immediately following the scene with Bobby. Begin the improvisation with "I just left Bobby and I . . . "

Improvise a scene with Tina playing the role of the person Bobby would turn to for help.

Following the improvisations share with your partner how your feelings for the characters have changed. How will you integrate this new learning into the scene?

Create a Working Set

Notes on Creating a Working Set

Encourage the students to transform boxes or platforms or chairs to create a set that suggests the space.

How will you create the world of the scene? Are they in a public place? What kind of public space? Decide where they are and how you will suggest this place. What sounds or soundscape would further develop the setting?

Find minimal set pieces to suggest this space.

Read through the scene again on the set with the necessary props. What would the characters have with them in the scene? How would they use these props to further suggest the setting?

Rehearsing/Presenting

There are a variety of ways to rehearse and present a scene. Many of the above activities and strategies are rehearsal techniques, and at times we use presentation activities during the rehearsal process to further prepare for a performance.

Below is one performance example that you may wish to try for this scene, and you can find even more options by turning to Performance Possibilities on page 177. You can also come up with your own strategies for presenting your scene using these examples as maps. Discuss with your partner or group which presentation strategy works best for your chosen scene.

Choose two snippets from the scene—one that has particular significance for Tina and one that has particular significance for Bobby—moments they will continue to think about after the scene. Each snippet should be four to six lines long and form a complete thought. For example, the lines beginning with Tina saying, "You have to start getting it together, Bobby! You really do," to Tina saying, "Because it might not happen." Rehearse the snippets with props on a set, in a designated space in the room. Decide which snippet will be first. Your decision may be made by the order in which it appears

Allow the students time after they have completed the monologue to highlight or choose the most important excerpt of the piece, something that would give the listener an idea of the characters' lives today. It can be effective to move from a Bobby reading to a Tina reading and to sometimes return to a student. Remind them to be prepared to read more than once.

Discuss the variety of responses following the reading and ask which situation the students think are most true to the characters.

in the scene or by character. Practise the transition from the first snippet to the second and present.

Reflecting

Writing in Role

Consider the future for Tina and Bobby. Do you think they will stay together? Will they separate? Will Bobby spend time with his daughter?

Write a monologue in the role of Tina or Bobby two years after the scene that addresses and begins to answer some of these questions.

Sharing the Monologues: Listening to the Voices

Create two images or tableaux, one representing Bobby and one representing Tina, with the images facing each other.

Without deciding on an order beforehand, read aloud an excerpt from your monologue on a signal from the instructor.

NOTES TO THE ACTORS AND DIRECTORS

This is a wonderful scene with two great characters with two very different motivations. What do Tina and Bobby want from each other? What happens when they don't get it? The research questions and the acting exercises suggested above will help you add depth to your performances. If you are playing Tina, you will want to know how difficult it is to live on social assistance. If you are performing Bobby, you will want to know how hard it is to get a job with no marketable skills. Try to interview someone who is or has been in those situations. Their words and feelings will make the situation real even if you have never experienced what Tina and Bobby are living through.

George F. Walker is one of Canada's most prolific and successful playwrights. He grew up in a working-class area of Toronto, an influence that can be seen in his plays. His career began in the early 1970s when he noticed a poster soliciting original scripts for the newly founded Factory Theatre. *Moss Park* premiered at Theatre Passe Muraille, Toronto, in 2014 in a co-production between Theatre Passe Muraille and Green Thumb Theatre, Vancouver.

READING AND RESEARCHING

Related Resources

Realizing Our Potential: Ontario's Poverty Reduction Strategy (2014–2019): www.ontario.ca/home-and-community/realizing-our-potential-poverty-reduction-strategy-2014-2019

Kids hit hardest by economic woes by Laurie Monsebraaten (Toronto Star): www.thestar.com/news/2007/03/06/kids_hit_hardest_by_economic_woes.html

Related Plays

Tough by George F. Walker

Jim and Shorty by Alex Poch-Goldin

Leaving Home; *Of the Fields, Lately*; and *Salt-Water Moon* (Three Mercer Plays) by David French

THE MIDDLE PLACE
BY ANDREW KUSHNIR

THE PLAY

The Middle Place is a play created from interviews with young people who were residents of the Youth Without Shelter youth shelter in Rexdale, Ontario, between 2007 and 2009. The words have not been altered by the playwright in any way. This process of playmaking is called verbatim theatre. Andrew Kushnir and his colleagues at Project Humanity were inspired to work in this fashion indirectly. They began with the desire to write a play about young people living in shelters to create empathy with a wider audience. What they found was that the young people's natural rhythms of speech (the pauses, word choices, the hiccups, the moments of flow) had a poetry and meaning that was more powerful than anything they could create themselves.

THE MONOLOGUE

There are two monologues in this excerpt, one from Aidan and one from Malik. The monologues come from questions being posed by the Outsider who, in the original production, spoke these lines from the audience. You can include the Outsider's lines (performed by another actor) or just focus on Aidan's and Malik's speeches alone.

THE CHARACTERS

Malik: A young black man in his early twenties. Malik has been in the shelter for three months. He works in a manufacturing plant but wants to get into modelling/acting. He says of himself that "I'm, I'm like, like the calmest guy till you just get on my last nerves like."

Aidan: A young white man in his early twenties. Aidan has been at the shelter for four years, on and off. He works in construction. He admits to having had issues with anger but that the caseworkers feel he's made great strides to manage them.

The Outsider: A white man in his late twenties. He is a playwright interviewing the residents for a play. He has no experience with a youth shelter prior to these interviews.

MONOLOGUE

OUTSIDER: What would be the ideal, like what are you looking for, like what would be . . . what would be a good date?

Beat. MALIK *scrunches his face.*

MALIK: A good date? It's, I don't know, everything goes nice, no argument, no nothing what-soever, an' the next date is the same thing, and the next date is the same thing again, just have a nice conversation, laugh, you know, share the same feelings or like, basically, yeah. Pretty much.

Long beat.

And not get *jealous*. Over little things, 'cause I actually met this one girl, she actually got jealous over everything. She even get jealous me talking to the next girl. Like, you know, and we just talking, you know, just having a conversation, and then she thinks it's nice for her talk to the next guy to make *me* jealous. I'm like, I'm like come on, you know. And I'm like and she fully wanted me to come live with her, right. I didn't like, even like, I stayed with her for like two days and like fff. *(kisses teeth)* And she already losin' it an' I'm like, "Whoa, god." You know. Like. So I just like, I don't like stupid games like that, you know.

OUTSIDER: Yah.

MALIK: *(laughs)* Somethin' like that. *(quick shift)* Let's just close that topic.

OUTSIDER: Yah yah, totally.

AIDAN *and the* OUTSIDER *alone.*

OUTSIDER: Aidan, can I ask how you and your girlfriend met?

AIDAN: Uh, through a shelter, actually.

OUTSIDER: Can you—is there a story behind that, or . . .

AIDAN: Um, *(shrug)* not really.

OUTSIDER: *(laugh)* You met at a shelter . . .

AIDAN: Yah.

OUTSIDER: Um . . .

Beat.

AIDAN: I walked in—it was Horizons, I was there I think six and a half, seven and a half months ago, I walked in and I was just pissed at everybody. And out of everybody in that shelter, she seemed to be the only face that lit up to me, so I walked over and then we just clicked from there.

OUTSIDER: Um, were you able to share your stories and sort of—

AIDAN: Yah.

Beat.

OUTSIDER: —um . . .

AIDAN: Like kind of—it felt like, to tell you the truth, we kind of connected right off the hop and, that's pretty much how it happened and we've been going every since. Like don't get me wrong, it's not lovey-dovey all the time, we fight like an old married couple and we've only been together six months, but when it all comes down to it, she's the only girl I want to spend the rest of my life with, and I'm gonna be willing to do anything to make it that way.

OUTSIDER: Cool. Um—

AIDAN: And it's weird, 'cause like you don't hear very many people—like if my kids ask me, I don't know what I'm gonna tell them, I met her in a shelter.

OUTSIDER: Well maybe that's part of relaying your experience and teaching them—

AIDAN: Mm-hm. But it's also what I'm thinking, like so Dad came from a shelter, but now he's a carpenter making forty-five bucks an hour, so if he can go from the dumps to something . . . then we're okay, you know what I mean? That might help my kids sleep better at the end of the night, okay well, so Dad was in a shelter, but now look at him. We've got a house, a big backyard, dogs and we have nothing to worry about. There's enough food in the fridge . . .

NOTES TO THE ACTORS AND DIRECTORS

These monologues are different from all the other scenes in this book. The other scenes came from the playwright's imagination. These monologues have been transcribed from interviews with real people.

The challenge to the actor is to recreate the speeches with the same spontaneity. They shouldn't sound like speeches but like the real people they are. Avoid any television stereotypes of how young people act and speak. For you to inspire empathy in the audience, you must have respect for the voice you are portraying. Pay particular attention to the punctuation and stage directions. Each period, comma, and ellipsis (. . .) has been carefully chosen to help you recreate the speech precisely as it was originally spoken.

For further strategies to explore and rehearse the monologue, turn to the Monologue Map on page 179.

PLAYWRIGHT AND PRODUCTIONS

The Middle Place was produced by Project: Humanity in 2009 at the SummerWorks Theatre Festival. The play then toured high schools and had its official world premiere in 2011 in a co-production between Project: Humanity, Theatre Passe Muraille, and the Canadian Stage Company. The play won the inaugural Toronto Theatre Critics' Award for Best Production.

BONE CAGE
BY CATHERINE BANKS

THE PLAY

Bone Cage explores the struggle of young adults striving to rise above the pillaged landscape of rural Nova Scotia. Through dark poetry and wry humour, Banks creates a world where the characters have hearts trapped in the bone cage of their own bodies, hearts that are desperate to break free.

THE MONOLOGUE

In this speech, Chicky tells the story of a sexual encounter with a much older, married man.

THE CHARACTER

Chicky: Twenty-five years old, works on the sod fields.

MONOLOGUE

CHICKY: The summer I turned fifteen I did something that people who knew me then would never have believed. It happened at the river. He'd brought a bunch of us swimming 'cause we were haying all day, and hot. Us girls were swimming in our shorts and white T-shirts so our bras would show through. The boys swam through our legs grabbing our crotches saying it was an accident; they was "stuck" or "drowning, honest to fucking God." He sat on the beach smoking, watching me like he had all summer. It was the first time I felt that feeling in my nipples.

He said he needed to see Clarence so he'd drop me off last. Then he asked and I said, "Yes, okay," and he took me back to the river. He brought me down to the water and he said he didn't have any right, he was a married man with kids even. He said I was so beautiful, and he wasn't trying to start anything up with me because that kind of man disgusted him, but he needed me to know that he loved me. And just saying it helped him so much and if he could once in a while tell me that, he'd be okay—never happy now, but okay. Then he stood up and he was walking up the bank. I knew how to stop him. I took off my T-shirt, my bra still damp from the river, and I said, "Reg!"

I did that, shy little me did that; I pulled him to me.

NOTES TO THE ACTORS AND DIRECTORS

This speech is darkly ironic in the sense that the character tells us this story to reveal something about herself, but what she actually tells us is something quite different. Who has the power in this situation? Chicky or Reg?

The language in this monologue is condensed and it is important that the actor flesh out the references more fully in her imagination. For example, a sentence like "It happened at the river" shows the character remembering a specific place. The actor could recreate this action by having a specific image in her mind for her to "remember." Give full weight to the punctuation. The playwright chose every comma and period the way a composer chooses rests and stops.

For further strategies to explore and rehearse the monologue, turn to the Monologue Map on page 179.

PLAYWRIGHT AND PRODUCTIONS

Catherine Banks is an award-winning playwright who lives in Sambro, Nova Scotia. *Bone Cage* was showcased at the National Arts Centre's On the Verge reading series in 2005, premiered in 2007 at the Neptune Studio in Halifax, and went on to win the Governor General's Literary Award for Drama in 2008.

TRUTH IN JUSTICE

TOUGH CASE
BY DAVID S. CRAIG

THE PLAY

Dane and his mother Marjorie have moved to a new town to escape an abusive father. On a dare, Dane and his new friends break into the home of Grace Ross, a retired librarian, and vandalize her home, which includes stabbing kitchen knives into the eyes of family pictures. Arrested and charged, Dane faces a conviction and the end of his dream of joining the armed forces until the judge suggests an alternative—restorative justice. Dane accepts without knowing what he is getting into and meets Nessa, a street-smart caseworker, who prepares him for a "conference" with Grace Ross and her vengeful son.

THE SCENE

Dane begins the scene with a short direct address to the audience that highlights his experience at a new school. He then rebels against his mother, and insists on going one on one with Nessa, his caseworker. Nessa discovers, through respectful but probing questions, that Dane has lived with an abusive father, is in trouble at school, has little guilt for his crime, and no remorse towards the victim, Grace Ross. Creating remorse and empathy is one of the central goals of restorative justice. Nessa finds one small chink in Dane's armour—a monogrammed pocket knife.

THE CHARACTERS

Dane: Sixteen.
Marjorie: Thirty-eight, Dane's mother.
Nessa: Twenty-six, a community justice worker.

CONNECTING WITH THE SCENE

Read the following quotations:

"When will our consciences grow so tender that we will act to prevent human misery rather than avenge it?" –Eleanor Roosevelt

"It is clear that the way to heal society of its violence . . . and lack of love is to replace the pyramid of domination with the circle of equality and respect." –Manitonquat

"The longer we listen to one another—with real attention—the more commonality we will find in all our lives. That is, if we are careful to exchange with one another life stories and not simply opinions." –Barbara Deming

"If you want to make peace with your enemy, you have to work with your enemy. Then he becomes your partner." –Nelson Mandela

"No future without forgiveness." –Bishop Desmond Tutu

Select the quotation that you would be prepared to defend, that you believe articulates your values as a member of your community, this city, the world.

Share this quotation with a partner and explain why you believe or hope it to be true in society today.

Can you think of a situation in your community where this value is currently not being upheld? Can you think of a situation in particular that relates to people in your age group. Share this situation with a partner.

SCENE

DANE speaks to the audience.

DANE: I didn't want to move down here. I knew I had to, but I didn't want to. I had friends in Fredericton. Guys I'd grown up with. Guys who'd watch my back. At this new school, everyone looks at me like I'm weird or looks through me like I'm invisible. I look weak and no one wants to talk to someone who looks weak because the weakness might be contagious, like a disease. You know what I'm talking about. Everyone in this room knows what I'm talking about, except no one talks about it.

MARJORIE: Dee-dee, sometimes I could just wring your neck.

DANE: Don't call me that. Call me Dane.

MARJORIE: Dee-dee's your name. Get used to it.

DANE: Does she have to be here?

NESSA: Yes.

MARJORIE: See.

NESSA: Unless you both agree.

DANE: We both agree.

MARJORIE: No we don't.

DANE: Yes we do. We agree. Right? Mum? We agree. Tell her.

MARJORIE: *(to NESSA)* I get the feeling he doesn't want me here.

NESSA: You have every right to stay, Marj.

MARJORIE: *(getting up)* It's okay. He wants to have some secrets from his old mom. Just don't be fooled by the tough guy stuff. He's a sweet boy. *(to DANE)* Right?

MARJORIE *exits.*

NESSA: Are you okay?

DANE: I'm fine—now.

NESSA: I mean about this restraining order on your dad.

DANE: It's no big deal.

NESSA: They don't give things these out for nothing.

   DANE shrugs.

I'm guessing they fought.

DANE: Oh yeah.

NESSA: How was that for you?

DANE: The fighting? The fighting was good. The fighting was what we wanted.

NESSA: Really?

DANE: Uh yeah. 'Cause when they were fighting, it meant that Mom was still talking and that meant she was still standing. It was when we couldn't hear her talk . . . that's when I wanted to go downstairs and stop him but Frank made me hide under the bed. 'Cause when Dad was finished with Mom, maybe he'd want to come upstairs and, you know, read us a bedtime story.

NESSA: You must be close to your brother.

DANE: He saved my life a million times.

NESSA: What was it like being scared in your own home?

DANE: No big deal.

NESSA: It would have been a big deal to me. Where I grew up, the fighting was outside on the street, not inside.

DANE: It's why I'm going to join the army. So I can protect myself.

NESSA: How do you like your new school?

DANE: It's a joke.

NESSA: How come?

DANE: Teachers don't like me.

NESSA: Why don't they like you?

DANE: 'Cause I tell the truth.

NESSA: Do you always tell the truth?

DANE: Yeah, and I'm the only one.

NESSA: Can you give me an example?

DANE: Only one? Ha!

NESSA waits.

Okay. At school they got these chairs, see. And they're hard. Like no human can sit on these chairs and be comfortable. So I have to stretch my feet out into the aisle, to be comfortable, and the teacher says, "Put your feet under the desk," and I say, "Why?" and he says, "Just do it," and I say, "What difference does it make where I put my feet? If I get the work done, why should it bother you?" And he says, "It doesn't matter why it bothers me, I'm telling you to put your feet under the desk." And I say, politely, "Screw you." And you know what he does? He sends me to the office!

NESSA: You said "screw you" to a teacher and you're surprised you got sent to the office?

DANE: See? You don't get it. I got punished because I told the truth.

NESSA: Well I'm glad telling the truth is so important to you, Dane. It's important to me too. But how you tell the truth is also important.

DANE: I didn't yell at him! I didn't punch him in the face!

NESSA: Okay, okay, okay. Let's try an experiment. Let's say, right now, I asked you to take down your hoodie and sit up straight, what would you say?

DANE: I'd say no.

NESSA: Why?

DANE: Because I'm more comfortable like this.

NESSA: And you think that's okay 'cause you're telling the truth.

DANE: Right.

NESSA: Okay. I get it. But here's the thing. You're not at home where you can do what you want. You're in restorative justice because of what you did to Grace Ross's home. And in restorative justice you have to be respectful. Here, with me, so I know you can do it, and then at the meeting with Mrs. Ross if she decides to come. The way you're sitting now? It's not respectful.

DANE: Says who?

NESSA: Says me. I'm in charge, just like the teacher in your class was in charge, and I'm saying, "Please, Dane, show respect for the process by taking down your hoodie and sitting up."

DANE: No.

NESSA: Then I guess you're not serious about joining the army, 'cause that place is all about respect.

DANE takes down his hoodie.

Good, Dane. That's not me winning. That's you being smart.

DANE: I don't know what the big deal is. We didn't burn the place down.

NESSA: That's true.

DANE: The place got messed up a bit. So what? She's got insurance.

NESSA: Insurance won't replace her family pictures.

DANE: She should get new pictures. The ones she had were really old.

NESSA: Really.

DANE: Black and white.

NESSA: Did you notice that before or after you stabbed the eyes out?

DANE: That was the other guys.

NESSA: Grace Ross is too frightened to sleep in her own house.

DANE: So? What am I supposed to do about that?

NESSA: I dunno. What could you do?

DANE: I'm not saying sorry.

NESSA: Why not?

DANE: 'Cause people say sorry all the time and they don't mean it.

NESSA: When I say sorry, I mean it.

DANE: You live in a nice world.

NESSA: I live in the same world you do, Dane. A world where people try not to hurt each other.

DANE: Ha!

NESSA: What if someone broke into your home and took your stuff?

DANE: I wouldn't care.

NESSA: There's not one thing you care about?

DANE: When you move on a bus you don't carry much.

NESSA: What about your knife? The one your brother gave you.

DANE: That's different.

NESSA: What's different about it?

DANE: It's got my initials on the blade.

NESSA: So it's special. Can you imagine Grace Ross walking into her home and seeing all her special things broken?

DANE: You're just trying to make me feel bad.

NESSA: Feeling bad is normal, Dane. It's what happens when you do something wrong.

DANE: Well it's not working. Stuff happens. Big deal. Get over it.

NESSA: Is that something your dad used to say?

DANE: Shut up.

NESSA: Did he say that too?

They stare at each other.

DANE: When do I get my knife back?

NESSA: Excuse me?

DANE: The police took it.

NESSA: So?

DANE: I want it back.

NESSA: Why should I do that for you?

DANE: 'Cause it's your job.

NESSA: Getting your knife back? That's not my job. Call the cops.

DANE: I tried, they said it was evidence.

NESSA: Oh. So you need me.

DANE: Forget it.

NESSA: Not so fast. I'll help you get your knife back if you do something for me.

DANE: What?

NESSA: I want you to pretend this coffee cup is your knife.

DANE: Why?

NESSA: It's a deal. Look at the coffee cup and pretend it's your knife.

DANE takes the cup.

DANE: This is stupid.

NESSA: Okay.

NESSA reaches for the cup. DANE pulls it away.

DANE: No.

NESSA: Then describe it. I don't have all day.

DANE: Okay. It's a Cold Steel Spartan flip knife with a four-and-a-half-inch blade.

NESSA: Should I be impressed?

DANE: Yes. It's made from Japanese AUS-8A stainless steel, and it's sharp, like a samurai sword, 'cause Frank sharpened it on a stone. You could split a hair with that knife.

NESSA: Is that what makes it special? Its sharpness?

DANE: No. Frank bought two knives—identical—and then he engraved our initials on the blade. His on one side. Mine on the other.

NESSA: Was it a birthday present?

DANE: No. He gave it to me the night before he went overseas.

NESSA: Can I hold it?

DANE passes the cup. NESSA crushes it.

DANE: Hey!

NESSA: What's your problem? It's just a knife. Get another one.

They stare at each other.

NESSA: Good work.

DANE: Are we finished here?

NESSA: Finished? No. We've just started. Here's your homework.

DANE: What?!

NESSA: I want you to write down how you think Grace Ross felt when she walked into her house and saw your reno. I'm going to meet with her son tomorrow to find out how she really felt. When you come back next week we'll see how close you get.

They have moved into the waiting area. MARJORIE stands.

MARJORIE: He has to come back again?

NESSA: Yes.

MARJORIE: Why? Did he give you a hard time?

DANE: *(walking past her)* Shut up.

MARJORIE: Hey. What happened to respect for your mother? *(to NESSA)* See what I have to deal with? If I have to come back next week I'll miss another shift. I can't afford that.

NESSA: He needs to come back because of what he did to Grace Ross's house, and because he's a minor you have to come with him.

MARJORIE: Well that's just great. Who's being punished here? Him or me?

Exploring Meaning

Text Play

Read the scene silently to yourself.

Read the scene out loud in a group of three.

Change roles and read the scene together again.

Read the scene sitting back to back in a small circle.

Notes on Text Play

Following each of these activities, ask the students to consider how the new reading has informed their understanding of the characters and to share the new learning with their partners or with the class.

Encourage the students to continue to switch parts to become familiar with all three characters. Only after significant exploration, invite the students to make a choice of which character to play for rehearsal and/or presentation.

Read the scene as Dane, avoiding any eye contact and looking anywhere but at Marjorie and Nessa. Read with Nessa and Marjorie trying to make eye contact with Dane.

Omit Marjorie for the following activities. Take turns reading and playing the roles of Nessa and Dane.

Read the scene facing each other and every two or three lines switch roles and continue reading.

Change roles and read the scene while walking together.

Read the scene quickly, loudly, slowly, again changing roles as you work.

Read the text, inserting a pause at some point in each line.

Read the scene without any pauses between the lines, saying your line immediately after your partner finishes their line.

Discuss with your partner which, if any, of these actions feel right for your character and adds to their portrayal.

Continue to change roles.

Negotiate and select the role you will play in the scene. The role of Marjorie is less developed, appearing only at the beginning and end of the scene. You will need to find other suggestions for how her role might be further developed. We suggest the actor who takes on the role of Marjorie also take on the role of the director at several points in the exploration.

Questions

What five things do you know for sure about the scene and characters?

Notes on Questions

Discuss with the students the difference between what we know for sure in a scene and what we think we know or assume.

What five unanswered questions do you have about the scene and characters? Is there anything from the scene or about the characters you wonder about?

Document your responses, rereading the scene if needed.

Share with a partner, group, or the whole class, noting similarities and differences between the questions.

Building Authentic Characters and Relationships

What I Don't Know About You!

Out of Role

Notes on What I Don't Know About You!

Encourage the students to be thoughtful in their choices of questions, looking for depth of understanding.

Begin out of role in your group of three. Consider some things you don't know about your partners that might give you a better understanding of them. You may want to know about their family or their interests. State three things you don't know about your partners and your partners will choose one of the three to discuss and share with you.

In Role

Repeat the activity in the role of your character. Nessa may want to know what Dane does when he gets home from school or which subject he enjoys.

Consider the questions that will give you further insight into the character. Again, the character should choose to answer only one of the questions.

Discuss in your group what you have learned about the characters from this exercise that will strengthen your portrayals of the characters.

I Don't Believe You!

Play the scene again. Any time you feel the character isn't truly in role and focused, you can stop the action and say, "I don't believe you!" The character will then repeat the line in a more convincing manner. The actor playing Marjorie can remain and continue to call out "I don't believe you" in the role of the director of the scene.

Notes on I Don't Believe You!

Students will have fun with this activity. Encourage them to listen and to be thoughtful about when to stop the action.

Consider how you might change the delivery of the line to be more believable, thinking about gesture, tone, volume, emotion, etc.

Discuss with your group how you continued to develop your role through the activity. What insights did you gain into the character and scene?

Try this activity again when you are working on the set.

Improvisation Flash Forward

Improvisation Flash Forward Notes

This activity will encourage students to consider the interview process, the skills of the interviewer, and the challenges of this position.

Move the drama forward to the moment after the scene. Nessa and Dane will meet with Nessa's supervisor to go over the interview. The student who played Marjorie will play the role of the supervisor.

To begin the scene, Nessa and Dane should give their feedback and perspective on the interview. The supervisor can ask further questions to learn more about the case and how it is proceeding. Begin with Nessa commenting on how she felt about the interview.

Create a Working Set

Notes on Creating a Working Set

Students can create a working set for their scenes as they rehearse. Discuss with the students how they can find costumes, props, and blocking clues in the text.

How will you create the office where the characters are meeting? Read through the script again, looking for clues as to what would be in the room, how the chairs might be set up, and their proximity to each other.

Also look closely at the text to find costume and blocking clues.

Read through the scene again on the set, moving through the space (blocking) and using necessary props.

Rehearsing/Presenting

There are a variety of ways to rehearse and present a scene. Many of the above activities and strategies are rehearsal techniques, and at times we use presentation activities during the rehearsal process to further prepare for a performance.

Below is one performance example that you may wish to try for this scene, and you can find even more options by turning to Performance Possibilities on page 177. You can also come up with your own strategies for presenting your scene using these examples as maps. Discuss with your partner or group which presentation strategy works best for your chosen scene.

Choose a section of the scene to present between Nessa and Dane. Bring Marjorie into the scene to listen, to comment at times, or to just physically respond to the conversation. You can decide if she is visible to Nessa and Dane, and then decide on her function. What actions or words will she bring to the scene? Rehearse and present, incorporating this new knowledge into the scene.

Reflecting

Building Empathy For Grace

As part of the restorative justice process, Nessa asks Dane to describe in writing how Grace Ross might have felt when she walked into her house after he and his friends had vandalized it. In the role of Dane, write out what you think he wrote for the next session.

Notes on Building Empathy

In this activity, students are encouraged to learn more about empathy and the importance of empathy in our lives.

The first activity would encourage Dane to find empathy for Grace and to understand the impact of his actions.

Students can share the excerpts with their partners or they could choose an excerpt to share with the class.

This activity could lead to a discussion of subtext and why we sometimes are unable to say what we are really thinking and feeling in the moment.

Imagine that Grace wrote her feelings down when she walked into her home. In the role of Grace write out your thoughts and feelings when you walked into the room and saw your house vandalized.

Select and share an excerpt from the writing that you think would most effectively develop this empathy for Grace.

Building Empathy For Dane

Select a few consecutive lines from the scene that you think most effectively creates empathy for Dane. This snippet would perhaps help Grace to better understand Dane and help her to decide to meet with him and negotiate a plan for Dane to make amends for his actions.

Share your scenes and explain the reasons for your choice. What will Grace see and learn through the scene?

Meeting Justice

Discuss with your group how Dane could repair the harm he has created. Describe a fair punishment for his crime. Share your ideas with the other groups. Would incarceration be an option?

NOTES TO THE ACTORS AND DIRECTORS

This is a dramatic scene, but it is also very static. It takes place in an office. Everyone is sitting in chairs. There isn't much opportunity for movement. The scene can be played successfully as written, but consider using your imagination to add something theatrical. For example, the dialogue and the characters are real but the set could be unreal, like an extremely small room to accentuate the tension. When Dane is talking about his teacher, his father, his brother, what if these off-stage characters appeared, visible only to Dane (and the audience)? Contrasting elements that are real with ones that are unreal and theatrical can add an enormous amount to this or any scene.

PLAYWRIGHT AND PRODUCTIONS

David S. Craig has written for theatre, radio, film, and television, but he is best known for his more than twenty plays for young people of all ages. *Tough Case* was commissioned by Professor Jennifer Llewellyn, director of the Nova Scotia Restorative Justice Community University Research Alliance. Nova Scotia has the largest restorative justice program in North America and the second largest in the world. The play was first produced by Left Foot First Productions in Halifax in 2011 and subsequently by Roseneath Theatre, Toronto, and the Manitoba Theatre for Young People in Winnipeg.

READING AND RESEARCHING

Related Resources

Tri-County Restorative Justice is a community-based, not-for-profit organization located in Yarmouth, Nova Scotia. It has plenty of information about bringing restorative justice programs into schools: www.tricountyrestorativejustice.com/

The International Institute for Restorative Practices Graduate School (IIRP) has been an integral part of a worldwide movement of scholars, policy-makers, and practitioners advancing the fields of restorative justice and, more broadly, restorative practices. Their website provides a wealth of knowledge on all matters concerning restorative justice: www.iirp.org/

The homepage for the Nova Scotia Restorative Justice Program, which includes links to further public education and research materials regarding the subject: www.gov.ns.ca/just/rj/

The homepage for the Nova Scotia Restorative Justice Community University Research Alliance, a partnership between university and community partners that focuses on research related to the institutionalization of restorative justice practice with particular attention to the example of the Nova Scotia Restorative Justice Program: www.nsrj-cura.ca/home

Community Justice Society—Halifax Region is an organization committed to offering programs and services to persons at risk or in conflict with the law: www.communityjusticesociety.org

The Fire Alarm, a YouTube video illustrating a restorative justice circle in practice with high-school students:
www.youtube.com/watch?v=WM2Cs0Qzn4Q

The Knife is another video example of a restorative justice circle:
www.youtube.com/watch?v=UUKHWhTBNA8

Related Plays

Innocence Lost: A Play about Steven Truscott by Beverley Cooper

Smokescreen by David S. Craig

Toronto the Good by Andrew Moodie

Wrecked by Chris Craddock

KIM'S CONVENIENCE
BY INS CHOI

THE PLAY

Mr. Kim is a first-generation immigrant from North Korea and the proud owner of Kim's Convenience, a variety store located in Toronto's Regent Park neighbourhood. As the area gentrifies, Mr. Kim is offered a generous sum of money to sell—enough to allow him and his wife to finally retire. But Kim's Convenience is more than just his livelihood—it is his legacy.

THE SCENE

In this scene, Mr. Kim is determined to convince his daughter Janet, a budding photographer, to take over his convenience store.

THE CHARACTERS

Appa (Mr. Kim): A fifty-nine-year-old first-generation Korean Canadian man, and owner of Kim's Convenience. He speaks with a thick Korean Canadian accent.

Janet: A thirty-year-old second-generation Korean Canadian woman. She is Appa and Umma's daughter.

Umma (Mrs. Kim): A fifty-six-year-old first-generation Korean Canadian woman. She speaks with a thick Korean Canadian accent.

CONNECTING WITH THE SCENE

On a notecard record:

Your favourite candy to buy at a convenience store.

The last time you went to a convenience store and the items you purchased.

If you've ever worked in a convenience store. If you have, write a note or two about what you liked about the work and what was the most challenging part of the job.

What you call your parents. (Mommy, Mamon, Mama, etc.)

What you call your grandparents.

Your parents' current or previous jobs.

Would you want to follow in your parents' footsteps? Explain why or why not.

What you think your parents want you to do when you leave school.

What you want to do when you leave school.

Select one item on your card to share with a partner.

Select and share one other item from your card with your partner. Share an item from your card with the whole class.

SCENE

APPA is offstage, returning from the back of the store while talking on the phone.

APPA: No, it's Christie—

ALEX: I'll pick you up in ten minutes.

ALEX exits. Bell. JANET returns behind the counter and begins to put on some makeup.

APPA: —then Bathurst, then Spadina, St. George, Bay, Yonge, Sherbourne, then is Castle Frank. Yah, one hundred percent guarantee. Yah, okay.

APPA hangs up the phone.

아이씨 바보. [Idiot.]

APPA pulls out JANET's Day-Timer and reads from it.

Okay, Janet, lesson number two: "Old is cold, new out of view." Old can is cold can, put in front. New can is not cold can, put out of view. "Old is cold, new out of view."

JANET: Appa, where'd you find that?

APPA: Upstair washroom.

JANET: I've been looking for that. Give it to me.

APPA: Wait, lesson number three is—

JANET: Appa, I gotta go.

APPA: Wait, we have to finish training, I make list—

JANET: Appa, I'm not taking over the store.

APPA: Janet, you is thirty years old now and still single. You have to understand, now is desperation time for you. Sudden death, overtime, penalty kick shootout. Expiration date is over. Take over store is only choice you having.

JANET: I can't believe—

APPA: Me and Umma is struggle whole life make life for you. We do what we have to do, hope you can be doctor, lawyer, big success, but what you do? Take picture. We don't have to come to Canada for you take picture. Even you can take picture in North Korea.

JANET: Appa—

APPA: Janet, I am dying . . . one day in future and before I dying, I—

JANET: You want to retire.

APPA: What is my story? Hm? What is story of me, Mr. Kim? My whole life is this store. Everybody know this store, they know me. This store is my story. And if I just sell store, then my story is over. Who is Mr. Kim? Nobody know that. You take over store, my story keep going.

JANET: But, Appa, that's life. Whether you choose it or get thrown into it, you make it what it is. And if you're not happy with your life, I'm sorry, but you can't expect me to make your life—I don't know—meaningful.

APPA: But I give my life, my story for you.

JANET: But you're the parent. You're supposed to.

APPA: Why is that supposed to? I don't have to give to you my life. I could throw you away as baby. I don't have to love you as baby, but I do. That is choosing. I choose like that. So, you have to be thank you and give to me you life. Second half. Fifty-fifty. That's fair. Yah, lookit, I am work at store, what you do, you don't work at store and still you eat, sleep upstair, yah? You whole life, that's how we doing. Thirty years. So, just switch side now, like soccer. Second half, you work at store and I don't work at store and still I eat, sleep upstair. Understand?

Beat.

I'm not live more than ten years, it's good deal for you.

JANET: That's a messed-up idea, Appa.

APPA: What you talking?

JANET: That's a seriously messed-up idea.

APPA: YOU seriously messed up—

JANET: No, Appa, that's—

APPA: YOU no.

JANET: No, Appa, really—

APPA: YOU really.

JANET: Stop doing that!

APPA: YOU stop.

JANET: Give me my Day-Timer, Appa!

APPA: Take out garbage and I give to you.

JANET ties the garbage bag to take it out.

What you doing?

APPA unties what JANET has done and ties it his way.

Have to roll like this. Push out air. Make tight. Small package. Then tie round back. That's best way.

APPA offers it to JANET. JANET takes it and unties what APPA has done and reties it.

JANET: That's your way. And if it matters that much to you, then do it yourself.

APPA: Janet, that's you job.

JANET: My job? I haven't taken out the garbage in sixteen years. All of a sudden it's my job again? Fine. But it wasn't even my job back then, 'cause if it were my job, then I would've gotten paid. So, what in fact I did back then and am doing right now is a favour for you. I wish you would at least appreciate this favour I'm doing for you, Appa.

JANET leaves with the garbage bag. Bell.

APPA: You pay rent? You pay for food?

APPA follows JANET.

What you talking? Take picture. Take picture! What's that?! Waste!!!

JANET returns with the garbage bag. Bell.

JANET: For my whole life, I've worked at least four hours a day covering for you guys, and I've never asked you for anything in return. I've never complained about it and never bitched about not getting paid. I've been here for you for my whole life, Appa. When Jung left, I was here. When Umma was sick, I was here. What would be nice is a simple thank you. A little appreciation, that's all I need. To hear you say "thank you." Just once.

APPA remains silent. JANET drops the garbage bag.

Okay, fine.

She goes behind the counter, takes out the printing calculator, and punches in the numbers.

Four hours a day, six days a week, fifty-two weeks a year, for the past twenty years, eight dollars an hour—subtract room and board . . . You owe me a grand total of $102,720! Give me my money, Appa!

Beat.

APPA: Piano lesson. Piano lesson. $20 every lesson. Once a week. Every week. Five years. I pay.

JANET tallies it up.

Golf lesson. $500. I invest in you.

JANET tallies it up.

Summer art camp. Material fee. $200. Every year.

JANET tallies it up.

Winter church camp. $100. Blue Mountain ski pass—

JANET: Wait.

APPA: Blue Mountain ski pass. $50. Grade 8 semi-formal dress—

JANET: Wait.

APPA: Prom dress—

JANET: Wait!

APPA: Diet program. Dating program. Orthodontist.

JANET stops tallying the numbers.

Computer. Camera. Hand phone. Tuition fee. Trip to Korea. TTC Metropass. Weight-losing program. Internet. Shoes. Clothes. Haircut. Everything you have Appa give to you. All Appa having, Appa invest to you and what you doing? Waste time. Waste money. Waste hope. What I still owe to you? Tell to me, Janet. I give to you my whole life, what fucking I still owe to you!?

Beat.

JANET: My Day-Timer.

APPA hurls the Day-Timer at the front door.

APPA: Ahhhhhh!

JANET slowly gets the Day-Timer and walks out. Bell.

Beat. Bell. UMMA returns.

UMMA: 아이고, 내성신콤뷔. 맨늴 이랜, 맨늴. [Oh my goodness, look at me, always forgetting things, always.]

UMMA takes an envelope from underneath the tray in the cash register. Beat.

왜 그랜요? 뮌일있어옵? [What's wrong? What is it?]

APPA: 아 니야. [Never mind.]

UMMA: 여보? 여보? [Honey? Honey?]

APPA exits to the back.

Exploring Meaning

Let's Make a
Convenience Store
Notes

This is a fun and
fast-moving game that
will engage students
with a variety of people
in the class. The game
will also encourage the
students to think about
the set for this scene,
which takes place in
Kim's store. You may
wish to use the game to
create working partners
for the scene study.

Let's Make a Convenience Store

Move through the space in a variety of ways: quickly, slowly, changing levels, etc. On a signal from the instructor create and remember the given image, where you created it, and who was in the image with you:

Alone: Your favourite candy.

A group of two: a popsicle.

A group of three: a bag of chips.

A group of four: a refrigerator display.

A group of five: the cash register and counter.

Whole class: the whole store.

Once students have created the items, the game is repeated as the instructor randomly calls out items and students re-create the image in the space where they first created it and with the same people.

Notes on Text Play

Prior to reading aloud
and playing with the
text, invite the students
to discuss their ini-
tial observations and
understanding of the
characters to encour-
age a truthful playing of
Appa. Discourage the
students from playing to
stereotypes by focus-
ing on the accent. In
discussing initial obser-
vations, students will
explore the tensions in
the relationships stem-
ming from the immigrant
experience.

Following each of these
activities, ask the stu-
dents to consider how
the activity has informed
their understanding of
the character and to

Text Play

Read the scene silently to yourself.

Share with a partner what you observed and learned about the characters from the scene.

With the whole class, share three things you know for sure about Janet and three things you know for sure about Appa.

Share any questions you have about Janet and Appa.

share their new learning with their partners or with the class.

Encourage the students to continue to switch parts to become familiar with both characters. Only after significant exploration, invite the students to make a choice of which character to play for rehearsal and/or presentation.

In order to play the role of Appa truthfully, read the words and lines as they are written and do not think about accents. Appa's background and character will then emerge.

Read the scene out loud with a partner.

Change roles and read it again.

Read the scene together sitting back to back.

Read the scene while engaged in a physical action particular to the character. For example, as Janet, mime that you are taking photos, writing in your Day-Timer or checking your phone. As Appa, mime that you are doing something in the store such as counting change, taking inventory, sweeping the floor.

Discuss with your partner which of these actions, if any, feel right for your character and add to your portrayal of them.

Building Authentic Characters and Relationships

What Is My Story: Tableaux

Notes on What Is My Story: Tableaux

Discuss with the class the significance of Appa's line, "What is my story?" Ask the students to consider their parents' story or their own story, reflecting on the importance of knowing your own story and communicating it to better understand each other. In examining Appa's story, students will further develop their understanding of the immigrant experience.

Form groups of four or five with all of the other students playing Appa. Create similar groups of four or five with the students playing Janet.

Brainstorm "What Is My Story," considering past, present, and future events that have shaped or will continue to shape your character's story.

Create four tableaux or still images to share your character's story and to help the other character understand your thoughts and feelings. The final image should reflect your character's vision of the future.

The Appa groups present to the Janets and the Janet groups present to the Appas.

Following the presentations answer the following questions and discuss:

- What have you learned about the other character through the tableaux?
- How will this inform your character?
- Do you now feel differently about your character, and if so what has changed?
- How will this new learning change your performance?

Improvisation

What do we know about Umma? How do you think she feels about the store? What does she want for Janet?

Considering these questions, create a scene between Umma and Janet with your partner, enlisting the person who is playing Appa to now play the role of Umma.

Imagine that Janet has gone to her mother for advice after her fight with Appa, trying to understand a way to proceed with her father.

Decide where the scene will take place. Will they meet upstairs, or at a coffee shop?

Begin the scene on a signal from the instructor and continue in role until the instructor signals you to end.

How has the meeting with Umma deepened your understanding of both characters?

Create a Working Set

How will you create the store? Remembering back to the initial activities, transform your working space into a section of the store. Given what you know about the scene, what are the key areas of the store the characters inhabit?

Consider and find the props that Janet and Appa use in the scene.

Notes on Improvisation

Encourage the students to be respectful and thoughtful as they role-play the mother. Discourage sterotypes based solely accents.

Question the Janets following the improvisation so that the students might hear the different interpretations of the mother. Sample questions include: Was your mother sympathetic? Did she help you understand Appa's concerns and feelings? What advice did she offer? Ask which responses felt more truthful given what we know about Janet and Appa. This will again further develop the understanding of the immigrant experience.

Notes on Creating a Working Set

Students can create a working set for their scenes as they rehearse. As an exercise in designing a set, the class could build one working set incorporating available furniture and props. This would be an opportunity to discuss elements of staging design.

Read through the scene again on the set, moving through the space (blocking), and using the necessary props.

Rehearsing/Presenting

There are a variety of ways to rehearse and present a scene. Many of the above activities and strategies are rehearsal techniques, and at times we use presentation activities during the rehearsal process to further prepare for a performance.

Below is one performance example that you may wish to try for this scene, and you can find even more options by turning to Performance Possibilities on page 177. You can also come up with your own strategies for presenting your scene using these examples as maps. Discuss with your partner or group which presentation strategy works best for your chosen scene.

We have created one set together. Divide the scene into sections between the students so that each group has an opportunity to present a portion of the scene on the set. Students can rehearse their sections and then present together in the order of the scene.

Reflecting

A Line That Speaks to Me

Select one line from your part that you feel is a line that you might actually have said in your life or that you feel one of your parents might have expressed. Explain either to your partner or in writing why you chose this particular line.

Writing in Role: Uncovering the Subtext

Write a letter in the role of your character. For example, write a letter as Janet to Appa, or write a letter as Appa to Janet just moments after the scene ends. Begin the letter with, "This is what I want you to know . . ." and express thoughts and feelings that you wish you could have articulated during the scene but could not.

Notes on A Line That Speaks to Me

In this activity, students are encouraged to very deliberately make personal connections to the characters and themes of the scene. Students could share these lines with the class or write a response to be shared with only you.

Notes on Writing in Role: Uncovering The Subtext

Students can share the letters with their partners or they could choose an excerpt to share with the class. The students in the role of Appa could read their excerpts aloud individually on a signal from the instructor while the students in the role of Janet listen, with or without their eyes closed, and then the Janets could read aloud.

This activity could lead to a discussion of subtext and why we sometimes are unable to say what we are really thinking and feeling in the moment.

Share your letter with your partner, either reading it aloud or giving it to them to read silently.

NOTES TO THE ACTORS AND DIRECTORS

Mr. Kim has found a wonderful solution to the problem of his daughter Janet's future. It's so reasonable. Why wouldn't she accept it? True, she wants to be a photographer, but how realistic is that? She should be practical like him. She should take his excellent advice. She should take over his convenience store.

Sacrifice is a theme that runs underneath these lines. Mr. Kim's arguments seem old-fashioned to a modern ear, but they have deep roots. In his note included with the published play, the playwright talks about his father growing up in Japanese-occupied North Korea and walking through the mountains of the Korean peninsula to freedom. He talks about his mother growing up in an orphanage in South Korea. They came to Canada to create a better life for their children, and running a convenience store was a means to an end. What were some of the things they sacrificed on that journey? How does that sacrifice affect Mr. Kim's relationship with his daughter? How does it fuel this scene? Can a parent's care ever be repaid? Should it be?

You will notice that Appa (Mr. Kim) speaks with a strong Korean accent and at the end of the scene Appa and Umma (Mrs. Kim) speak in Korean. How does a non-Korean actor do this? Imitation! Find a Korean-speaking person and ask them to read the dialogue. Be sure to make a recording. Listen to the tape. Remember, you are only imitating the accent. The feeling and intention is yours.

PLAYWRIGHT AND PRODUCTIONS

Kim's Convenience was first produced by the playwright, Ins Choi, at the Toronto Fringe Festival in 2011 because he couldn't find an established theatre to produce it. This meant he had to find an audience, so he canvassed every Korean variety store and church he could find. His production won a Fringe New Play Award, an Audience Choice Award, and sold out the entire Fringe run and a subsequent extension. The play was remounted by the prestigious Soulpepper Theatre in 2012, where it played to full houses before moving on to a national tour.

Related Resources

Caught Between Two Cultures, a TVO discussion of the impact on children caught between two cultures: www.youtube.com/watch?v=ORog_-2ovz8

This CBC News piece features second-generation Canadians opening up about bullying at school and experiencing cultural conflict at home: www.cbc.ca/news/canada/children-of-immigrants-caught-between-2-cultures-1.1225779

Related Plays

A Brimful of Asha by Asha and Ravi Jain

Fronteras Americanas by Guillermo Verdecchia

Mom, Dad, I'm Living With A White Girl by Marty Chan

Letters To My Grandma by Anusree Roy

Leaving Home by David French

THE VALLEY
BY JOAN MacLEOD

THE PLAY

The Valley casts a simultaneously chilling and sympathetic eye on the challenges faced by family members when a loved one is suffering from a mental illness. The story revolves around two pairs of characters: Connor, eighteen, and his mother Sharon; and Dan and his wife Janie. The action moves fluidly back and forth between the couples as well as backwards and forwards through time.

Connor returns suddenly from his first term at university vowing never to return. His alienation from the real world increases until finally he is found walking through the car of a SkyTrain swinging a bicycle chain. Dan, a police officer, subdues him and, in the process, breaks Connor's jaw. Dan is untouched by his actions but his wife, who is suffering from postpartum depression, is drawn to Connor's story. Against Dan's wishes, she attends a reconciliation circle organized by Connor's mother before contemplating suicide to end her own suffering.

THE SCENES

The two scenes we have chosen focus on the relationship between Connor and his mother. The first occurs when Connor initially returns from university. The second takes place some weeks later.

THE CHARACTERS

Connor: Eighteen years old.
Sharon: Fifty years old, Connor's mother.

CONNECTING WITH THE SCENES

Agree or disagree with the following statements, noting your responses to each:

Adolescents have so much drama in their lives.

There is no reason for teenagers to be depressed.

Depression is just typical adolescent feelings and behaviours.

Depression affects girls more than boys.

People with depression can be cheered up by their friends.

There is a stigma attached to people with depression or other mental health problems.

There isn't anything we can do to help someone who is depressed.

We can learn how to help someone who is facing depression.

People who work really hard can overcome any obstacle, including depression.

Share your responses with a partner or with a small group. Return to these statements following the scene study. Have your responses changed?

Notes on Connecting With the Scene

This Anticipation Guide can be copied and handed to students to respond to individually and privately or as a tool for discussion with the whole class.

SCENES

Scene 1

CONNOR: I dropped Environmental Studies.

SHARON: Why?

CONNOR: And Philosophy. I wasn't . . . engaged.

SHARON: What does that mean?

CONNOR: It means it was all bullshit.

SHARON: Some of us didn't expect university to be entertaining. What are you taking instead of Philosophy and Environmental Studies?

CONNOR: Writing. And Astronomy.

SHARON: And English. I know that. What are you taking instead of Philosophy and Environmental Studies?

CONNOR: Nothing.

SHARON: You're only taking three courses?

CONNOR: Did I say I was taking three courses?

SHARON: Connor–

CONNOR: I dropped Environmental Studies. And Philosophy.

SHARON: You just said that.

CONNOR: And probably English. I'm thinking about dropping English.

SHARON: The novel study? Why would you do that? You couldn't wait to take that course–

CONNOR: *Tess pranced down the rosy country lane with her fluttering bosom fluttering!*

SHARON: Don't you dare make fun of Thomas Hardy! You know how much he means to me.

    Beat.

If you go down below three courses you'll lose your scholarship money.

CONNOR: The books are so boring and . . . I can't finish any of them. I can hardly start them.

SHARON: Your dad won't be able to keep you on his medical if you drop below three courses. And if you think I'll ever get benefits at my job, you're sadly mistaken.

CONNOR: It's not my fault that you work in a bookstore. You don't have to work there.

SHARON: The point is why this is happening in the first place. Why are you dropping courses?

CONNOR: I haven't dropped English yet. I just haven't been for a while.

SHARON: Connor. Talk to me. What's going on?

CONNOR: Nothing.

SHARON: Your dad said you were having some issues with your roommate.

CONNOR: I don't have issues. Ethan has issues.

SHARON: How is Creative Writing going? Did you show your professor your books?

CONNOR: He doesn't have time to read novels. He has 135 students. He doesn't even have time to mark our assignments. The TA marks them.

SHARON: Would it help if I dropped him a note, or I could—

CONNOR: You think I'm still in kindergarten.

SHARON: I'm just trying to figure out what happened to the young man who walked through the door six weeks ago and couldn't wait to start university. I'm really really concerned about you.

CONNOR: Adverbs are weak words. Did you know that? You use adverbs all the time. *Completely. Utterly. Abominably.*

SHARON: Stop it.

CONNOR: *Verily verily.* Jesus Christ was the King of the Adverbs. I'm going to tell that to Ethan-the-Mormon.

SHARON: Does your dad know you've dropped two courses? Connor. I'm talking to you—

CONNOR: I'm not going back.

SHARON: Excuse me?

CONNOR: You can't make me go back. I'll still get fifty percent on my tuition. I'll pay back everything I owe you. I mean it. Everything.

Pause.

I'm sorry, Mum.

SHARON: What happened?

CONNOR: Nothing happened!

SHARON: A normal person doesn't suddenly decide after looking forward to something for years and years to give up all of a sudden and—

CONNOR: I should've taken a year off. A lot of people I know are taking a year off. Paul's in Fort McMurray making like twenty bucks an hour. I could do that. I should've done something like that. Just for this year.

SHARON: Paul didn't finish high school. He doesn't have the options, the opportunities you have in front of you.

CONNOR: Or that government thing where you go do volunteer work. I could help Inuits. Or salmon. I could help . . . something.

SHARON: If you were interested in volunteering, if that was your goal, then you should have been applying to different agencies and you should've been doing so, undoubtedly, in the spring.

CONNOR: Undoubtedly. Impossibly. Irretrievably. Dementedly.

SHARON: This is ridiculous!

CONNOR: Finally.

   SHARON *begins to exit.*

Ethan takes stuff from me. Pens. Pages from my notebook. He knows the password for my computer.

SHARON: There must be someone at the residence that you can talk to about that.

CONNOR: I'm not going back.

SHARON: I'll fly back with you and help sort this out.

CONNOR: Every single night, as soon as I've gone to bed, Ethan phones his girlfriend and talks to her for hours and hours and hours.

SHARON: We'll try again to get you a single room.

CONNOR: Would you fucking listen to me for once? I'm not going back!

Scene 2

CONNOR is interrupted by a rapping on the door. Lights up on SHARON.

CONNOR: Fuck.

CONNOR closes his laptop.

SHARON: I appreciate that you're looking for work online, BUT there might be something tacked up in a window or in one of the weeklies that isn't on the computer BUT just may be the perfect job. You won't know about it though if you just keep holed up in your room.

Beat.

It's been nearly a month now.

Beat.

There's a BIG WIDE RAINY world out there!

Beat.

Connor? Could you please at least acknowledge that you are in your room? That you are listening? That I am not talking to a brick wall?

CONNOR: You are not talking to a brick wall.

SHARON: And perhaps your expectations given your lack of experience are a tiny bit high.

CONNOR flicks his joint away.

SHARON: Smoking grass every day isn't going to help either. Look, I know you are capable of doing anything you put your mind to. Anything. Both your dad and I feel that way. But maybe it would be a good idea to have a shower, put on some clean clothes, and talk to a counsellor—an employment counsellor. Maybe it would be a good idea to talk to a regular counsellor too—about Calgary, about your having to come home.

Pause.

Did you know that one in four university students experience prolonged periods of anxiety or depression? Especially young males. Especially in first year when it's their first time away from home. It isn't anything to be ashamed of.

There was a well-worn path between my residence and the counselling centre when I was at U of T. I took full advantage of—

CONNOR throws open the door.

CONNOR: If you tell me that you know how I feel, how THIS feels . . .

If you even insinuate for one second that you have a fucking clue what it's like to be me, here, now, living this shitty, stupid life. IF you try and do that one more time—I'm going to kill myself!

SHARON: DON'T say that!

CONNOR: I mean it.

SHARON: You say many many things to me. And sometimes they are hurtful, hateful things, but I know that deep down that it's . . . it's . . . AWESOME that we can have open communication, but you CANNOT SAY THAT to me.

CONNOR: Okay.

SHARON: Okay.

Pause.

CONNOR: In Calgary, when I got up to pee in the middle of the night—when I walked on the carpet down the hall—sparks came out from under my heels. I'm not kidding.

SHARON: That happened when we were in Jasper too—it's the dryness.

CONNOR: Then I'd go up on the roof of the residence, and even when it was pitch black . . . the air . . . the air was full of static. Charged up. And the Rockies—they would reveal themselves to me.

SHARON: What are you doing on the roof of the residence at night?

DIGGING DEEPER INTO THE SCENE

Exploring Meaning

Text Play

Read the scene silently to yourself.

Then read out loud with a partner.

Change roles and read it again.

Read the scene sitting back to back.

Read the scene walking beside each other and walking through the space.

Read the scene with Sharon trying to make eye contact and Connor trying to avoid eye contact.

Read the scene while constantly moving around the room and then being perfectly still.

Read the scene sitting or standing very close to each other and then a distance away.

Discuss with your partner which ways of reading the text felt most truthful to the characters and the situation.

Notes on Text Play

The two scenes in this study demonstrate the progression of Connor's depression and its impact on his life and on his mother. You could give one scene to half the class and the second scene to the other half of the class, or you could work with one scene with the whole class and then introduce the second scene for later work. The scenes do stand on their own.

Questions

What five things do you know for sure about the scene and characters?

What five unanswered questions do you have? Is there anything from the scene you wonder about?

Document your responses, rereading the scene if needed.

Share your questions with a partner, group, or the whole class, noting similarities and differences between your questions and others' questions.

Notes on Questions

Discuss with the students the difference between what we know for sure in a scene and what we think we know or assume.

Building Authentic Characters and Relationships

Hot Seat

Given the change in Connor since he went to university, whom might his mother want to speak with in order to better understand what has happened and how she might help him?

Generate a list of people in Connor's life who might be able to answer some of the questions from the above activity, his roommate, a professor, his father, etc. Consider people who might have known Connor before he went away who might have also noticed the change, such as friends.

Choose three or four characters from this list to interview and ask for volunteers to play these roles. You might interview the characters in small groups or as a whole group. Think of the questions that will uncover some of the answers to help Sharon and us better understand Connor's present thoughts and feelings.

When in the hot seat, use the information from the text and previous explorations to imagine what the character might know and be willing to share. You may choose not to answer a question in role if it is too personal to the character or if you are uncertain of how the character might answer. Stay in role even if you decide not to answer a question.

Hot Seat Notes

These activities would apply to either or both scenes.

Students could work in pairs, small groups, or as the whole class to look closely at the characters and their relationships in this activity.

You could model authentic role-play by first playing one of the roles in the hot seat yourself and inviting the class to interview you.

Following the hot seat, and out of role, discuss:

What did we learn about Connor?
How did the characters in the hot seat feel about Connor?
Do you believe everything they said?
Do you think they were withholding information?
What are their perspectives?
If you were Connor, whom would you trust in this group?

Objects of Character

Connor spends more and more time isolated in his room in the scene. At the beginning of the second scene, Sharon goes into his bedroom to speak with him. Think about and discuss how we might learn about a character or person by visiting their bedroom or personal space, seeing the important objects in their life and where they chose to place those objects.

Given what you know about Connor, bring in an object that he might have in his room and think of the story behind that object. Did someone give it to him? How and why might it be meaningful to him?

Share the story of the object with a partner.

Building Connor's Room

In silence, using the available props and furniture in the room and the objects from the previous activity, create Connor's bedroom. Negotiate in silence the placement of the furniture and objects, moving them both around until everyone is satisfied and a consensus is reached. Try to be respectful of the character and everyone's choices in the creation of the room.

When the bedroom (set) is complete, ask for volunteers to play Connor and his mom and decide together the positions they will take in the room as the scenes unfold, sitting or standing, close or far from each other, making eye contact or looking away.

Notes on Objects of Character

You might ask students to bring in an object or you could bring in objects that you feel describe Connor and ask the students to endow the objects with Connor's story.

Notes on Building Connor's Room

This activity is directly related to the second scene, but the learning can also inform the first scene.

Encourage the students to work in silence and negotiate respectfully as they place the objects. When you feel students have found consensus you might give them a signal to stop. Building the room and placing the characters in the room makes the work feel "real" and might trigger an emotional response in the students playing Connor and his mom. Consider whether you feel the students volunteering will be able to handle the roles and the possible responses.

Following this activity discuss what you learned about Connor through building his room.

- How do you feel about him now?
- What did you learn about his mom, Sharon?
- How do you feel about her?
- Describe a moment in the activity that stood out for you.

Create a Working Set

Create a working set for each scene. You could use or adapt Connor's bedroom from the previous activity to create the set for the first scene.

Read through both scenes again on the set with the necessary props.

Continue to rehearse on the set.

You might want to use Connor's bedroom to present the second scene.

Rehearsing/Presenting

There are a variety of ways to rehearse and present a scene. Many of the above activities and strategies are rehearsal techniques, and at times we use presentation activities during the rehearsal process to further prepare for a performance.

Below is one performance example that you may wish to try for this scene, and you can find even more options by turning to Performance Possibilities on page 177. You can also come up with your own strategies for presenting your scene using these examples as maps. Discuss with your partner or group which presentation strategy works best for your chosen scene.

If you have explored both scenes, you might want to select and present sections of each scene to closely examine the progression of Connor's mental health issues. Create a different set showing another part of their home for scene one and consider how you will make the transition from scene one to scene two.

Reflecting

The Space Between Us

Select a moment in the scene that you feel represents the essence of the piece. Create a physical image that shows the relationship between Connor and his mother in this moment, such as reaching out, turning away, speaking at a significant distance.

Notes on The Space Between Us

Record and discuss the words with the students following the activity. The words will represent the universal themes brought out in their work.

Think about a word that would describe this space between the two of you. Is it fear? Trust? Or something else?

In a carousel, share the images and words and record the words on a chart.

Discuss with your partner and the class how the characters could address these words and move forward together.

Agree or Disagree

Revisit the questions in Connecting With the Scene from the beginning of this piece. Have your thoughts changed through the work? To find out more about depression and mental health, access the resources below in Reading and Researching.

NOTES TO THE ACTORS AND DIRECTORS

In every family, everywhere, there are scenes between concerned mothers (or fathers) and defensive sons (or daughters). From this perspective, the scenes we have chosen from *The Valley* will be very familiar. But because we have all lived through some variation of these scenes, because it is so very "real," any overacting (or underacting!) will weaken the effect. One of the most important notes a director can give actors is to listen to each other. It sounds simple but it means you are not thinking of the line you are about to say, or anything else. You are listening, with complete focus, to what the other character is saying to you and allowing yourself to respond.

The tension between Connor and his mom comes from the feelings that each character is hiding. What are they? Are any of them the same? Why doesn't Sharon just stop asking questions? Why doesn't Connor just stop answering them?

Both scenes have rising conflicts. That means the tension rises as the playwright reveals new information. Go through the script and circle these points. What emotional impact does this new information have on the character? How does it affect your posture? Your breathing? The tone of your voice?

PLAYWRIGHT AND PRODUCTIONS

Joan MacLeod is one of Canada's most respected playwrights. Although *The Valley* had its first production at Alberta Theatre Projects in Calgary in 2013, she is closely associated with the Tarragon Theatre in Toronto, where she was playwright-in-residence for two years. Joan teaches playwriting at the University of Victoria. You can learn more about her at www.joanmacleod.com.

READING AND RESEARCHING

Related Resources

The website for the Centre for Addiction and Mental Health provides information about mental health issues and promotes environments that support positive mental health: www.camh.ca

The Anxiety Disorders Association of Canada website provides information on anxiety disorders, useful organizations, and other resources: www.anxietycanada.ca

Kids Help Phone provides information and counselling services for youth from the ages of five to twenty, available via the Internet and phone 24/7. Counselling and support is free, one to one, professional, confidential, and anonymous in both English and French: www.kidshelpphone.ca

Teen Mental Health provides resources, curriculum support, and information that promote mental health and well-being for teens: www.teenmentalhealth.org

Mood Disorders Society of Canada is a not-for-profit volunteer organization committed to improving quality of life for people affected by depression, bipolar disorder, and other related disorders: www.mooddisorderscanada.ca

Distress Centres Ontario provides telephone support for individuals experiencing mental health problems, emotional distress, and/or social isolation 24/7: www.dcontario.org

Caring Minds provides relevant, historical, and current material related to mental health: www.caringminds.ca

The American Foundation for Suicide Prevention's More Than Sad: Teen Depression, a YouTube series on adolescents and depression (PSA): www.youtube.com/watch?v=MiS02j3zt68, www.youtube.com/watch?v=bBl-xQjcDLw&feature=channe

In this TED Talk, Dr. Stephen Ilardi speaks about the symptoms of depression and strategies for recovery: www.youtube.com/watch?v=drv3BP0Fdi8

The Truth About Depression, BBC Documentary: www.youtube.com/watch?v=F5YubjEqbZ8

Workman Theatre Project, an arts and mental health company known internationally for its artistic collaborations, presentations, knowledge exchange, best practices, and research in the area of the impact of the arts on the quality of life of people living with mental illness and addiction: www.workmantheatre.com

Related Plays

The Little Years by John Mighton

That's Just Crazy Talk by Victoria Maxwell

God's Middle Name by Jennifer Overton

Heartwood by Laura Burke

LETTERS TO MY GRANDMA
BY ANUSREE ROY

THE PLAY

In *Letters To My Grandma*, a high-school student, Malobee, discovers letters detailing her grandmother's fight to survive the 1947 partition of India, which resonates with Malobee's own struggles to create a new life in present-day Toronto. An intimate multi-generational tale of hatred, regret, love, and forgiveness, *Letters To My Grandma* weaves the remarkable stories of these two women together, inextricably linking their histories and delving into how the hatred bred between Hindus and Muslims in the Old World consumes families in Canada today.

THE MONOLOGUE

Letters To My Grandma is a full-length one-person play. We have chosen two sections that reveal different facets of Malobee's character, and of her relationship with her grandmother. In the first section (scene five of the play), Malobee, a Hindu teenager, has just arrived in Canada. On one hand, she notices that Canadian society is more accepting of mixed-race relationships, but on the other she experiences racial stereotyping. The scene also establishes the deep love and respect Malobee has for her grandmother. In the second scene (scene nine in the play), Malobee tries to explain to her grandmother that she is in a romantic relationship with a Muslim boy.

THE CHARACTER

Malobee: Is full of love and fear. She is torn between loyalty to her family and her hope for happiness.

Monologue One

MALOBEE, eighteen, narrates a letter to her GRANDMA.

MALOBEE: Sricharaneshu Amma, bhalo accho?* Dear Amma, how are you? I got your letter last week. That took quite a while, ha? Three weeks since you posted it. You have to start using the phone more often, Amma, then we can talk more. I know you are angry, but Ma has said it a hundred times, Baba's job change was not his fault.

Beat.

Anyway, today is the thirteenth, one full year in this new country, ha? Ki tara tari time flies, na?† Bishshashi ei hoy na,‡ that it was just last year I wrote to you saying how much I hated the winter in Toronto. And now I can't wait for it to snow. It looks so beautiful outside. You can see the patterns of the flakes. Eai mone hoy kalkaye§ we landed in the airport, cold and wet in the rain, somehow managing to sleep all four of us on that one bed. I still feel new though, still like an immigrant. I don't know when or how that will change, but I know for now it's still there.

Beat.

Anyway, I have a teacher here, Mrs. Hardy. She is Indian, married to a white man. It is totally acceptable here. Whites marry blacks, Indians marry Chinese, probably cows marry chicken! But they still make fun of me though, calling me Paki, so I guess they are not *that* accepting, but don't worry, all the people who call me that are not my friends anyway. And I think the next time someone calls me that I will call them an *American* and then they will get my point.

Beat.

So Mrs. Hardy gave us an assignment for OAC English class; I have to write about the most influential person in my life, and of course I picked you. I have so many questions for you. Why didn't you tell me more about the war? Ma tells me these stories that you never told me

---

* Respected Amma, are you well?

† How quickly time flies, no?

‡ I cannot even believe that . . .

§ It feels like yesterday . . .

about. I don't even know what to ask. What was it like to be on that train with refugees? Ma said that Japan used to carpet bomb Burma and you had to steal from other people to eat? How did it feel when Dadai came back four years after the war, when you thought that he was dead and they made you wear widow's white. Did you hate him for that? All these years I have lived with you and now that I have moved far I am trying to get to know you. There is a lot of getting to know going on right now . . . there is a boy . . . he is nice. His name is Mark. I am getting to know him too.

I miss you, Amma. You and your stories. I love you so much. Please please please write to me. Bhalo theko, Bee.

P.S. Everyone here calls me Bee. Short form for Malobee. Pretty cool, na?

Monologue Two

MALOBEE dials GRANDMA's phone number.

MALOBEE: Hello. Is this Briddho old home? Hi. Can you connect me to room 14C please? Thank you.

Waits with anticipation.

Hi Amma. Kamon aacho,* you are doing well? Good. You still taking your Autrin? Good, good—

Ahh . . . So, there is something I umm . . . wanted to say. Ahh . . . remember how last week I told you that I have a really good friend, Mark? Yes, Mark. Umm . . . well, I wanted to say that I really like him.

Beat.

Like, he has become my special friend. He met Ma and Baba yesterday. Yes, for the first time. Well, they think he is okay. They want me to tell you first and . . .

Beat.

---

*   How are you?

Yes, yes, yes it is a good thing, right? It is a good thing. That's what I am trying to tell them. Because I am getting older. And . . . No no, he is not British. He is *not* British. But, umm . . . what I wanted to say was that, he umm . . . he calls himself Mark, but that's not his real name. That's like a nickname, right? You know how I say that people here call me "Bee" from Malobee. Ya. Umm . . . his real name is . . . Mohammed. Mohammed Ahmed.

Yes. Yes, he is Muslim. Yes, from Pakistan. But, but . . . but they are really progressive. Like like like his family is really progressive. And and and they believe in in in Islam and they are really good people. You know how you used to always say that in the war there were dirty Hindus and then there were good Hindus? Same thing, but these are good Muslims, Amma, and you will really really like him if you got to know him . . . do you want talk to him someday? You could talk to him and . . .

GRANDMA *has hung up.*

Hello? Hello? Amma? Hello?

Shit.

(to herself as she redials the number) It's okay. It's okay.

Waits for connection.

Hello. Hi. My line got disconnected. Could you connect me to room 14C again, please. Thank you.

Pause.

Tell her it's her daughter calling and she really needs to talk to her.

Pause.

Please please. Just just give her the phone.

Put the phone near her ear, just one more time, please.

Pause.

Can you just please try.

NO NO, listen. Hello.

They hang up.

Shit. Shit. Shit. Shit. Shit.

NOTES TO THE ACTORS AND DIRECTORS

Malobee is experiencing some intense and varied feelings in this monologue. She is dealing with a new language, a new country, and, most importantly, a new culture. Sometimes these experiences are exciting and sometimes they are not. In the first monologue, Malobee is trying to describe her new world to her grandmother in a letter. What is her approach? What effect does she want to have on her grandmother? These answers will colour your reading.

In the second monologue, the action is more immediate. She is talking directly to her grandmother. It is very important that you know what the grandmother is saying even though the audience will never hear those lines. Write them in your script. Be as concise as possible. When you rehearse or "run your lines" have someone play the grandmother and read her lines. When you perform the monologue, "hear" the grandmother speaking in the pauses. This will magically turn a one-sided telephone conversation into a real dialogue.

You will notice that there are a few words of Hindi in the text. This is an essential part of the scene because it makes the reality of the two cultures so apparent. Record someone who speaks Hindi reading the lines and practise saying them. You don't have to be perfect but you do need to be respectful.

For further strategies to explore and rehearse the monologue, turn to the Monologue Map on page 179.

PLAYWRIGHT AND PRODUCTIONS

Anusree Roy was born in Calcutta, India, in 1982. She immigrated to Canada with her family when she was seventeen. *Letters To My Grandma* premiered in 2009 at Theatre Passe Muraille in Toronto.

THE PLAY

Sunny, a.k.a. rihannaboi95, likes to make videos of himself as Rihanna—singing like her and looking like her—which is perhaps not what a traditional Muslim teenage boy is supposed to be doing in the shower. But who cares? His posts are popular on YouTube. Really popular. Until someone from his school notices and his creative world gets a cold, hard dose of intolerance. He runs away from home and takes refuge with Keira, "a Shoppers makeup queen," who gives him the opportunity to make one last video for his loyal followers.

THE MONOLOGUE

The monologue was originally written to be performed for audiences watching over the Internet, with the actor speaking into a camera. We feel it is effective without this technology, but if you have the time, add a camera and monitor so the audience can watch two realities at the same time—one real and one virtual.

THE CHARACTER

Sunny: A teenage boy who feels most comfortable imitating Rihanna.

MONOLOGUE

SUNNY: You have no idea how hard it was to make a video in my apartment, everyone living on top of each other, King always getting up in my bidness. So I had to plan it out. The only time my family left the apartment was Saturdays when we visited Auntie, who's like not even my real auntie but some old family friend, and we always had to go once a week. So like that morning I pretended I was sick, soup can into the toilet, you know, so Mom let me sleep when they went. The second they left I jumped outta bed 'cause I knew I only had like two hours. I set the laptop up in front of the bathtub 'cause we have this shower curtain with all these flowers on it that look kinda like the ones from Rihanna's video and, like, if I leaned back on the curtain like this it looked like I was lying back on the flowers like she did. And I strung these blinking Christmas lights I got from Dollarama along the curtain rod to be the fireworks and wrapped our tablecloth around me and put on this headband and used half of Mom's lipstick until it was so thick I thought my lips would collapse. And I'd watched the video so many times that I had it memorized. I pressed record, climbed into the tub, and began singing to it in my head and doing the moves, exactly like Rihanna did, like so specific, singing right to Mr. Bailey in his car.

And suddenly there's banging on the door. I slipped back and grabbed the curtain rod but it gave out and I smashed my head against the fucking tiles, all the Christmas lights falling on me. I heard King's voice: "I need to piss." And I just yanked the shower on and shouted, "I'm in the shower!" He said, "I need to go, unlock the door." I felt blood all over the back of my head and the smashed lights cutting my back. I unplugged them so I wouldn't fry myself and pulled off the white cloth and tried rubbing the lipstick off but it just smudged all over my face. "One second!" I stumbled out of the shower and stuffed the laptop under the sink and tried fixing the curtain rod back into place but King was pounding on the door now. "What are you doing in there, jerking off?" I got the curtain back up and flicked open the lock and jumped back behind the curtain, my feet landing on the smashed lights. I bit my lip, like *wallahi* so much pain. I heard King over by the toilet beginning to piss. "What happened to the curtain?" he said. "You were rushing me, I slipped." I watched my blood swirling down the drain as I was trying not to cry. King walked over to the sink and said, "What's Mom's lipstick doing here?" My heart jumped into my throat. The lipstick. Fuck. I pretended not to hear. "Sunny?" My eyes were closed, I said nothing. "Make sure you fix that curtain, okay?" And then he left.

NOTES TO THE ACTORS AND DIRECTORS

Who is Sunny talking to in this monologue? Why is he telling the story? Why is he telling it now? What mood is he in when he begins speaking? What mood is he in at the end?

For further strategies to explore and rehearse the monologue, turn to the Monologue Map on page 179.

PLAYWRIGHT AND PRODUCTIONS

Jordan Tannahill is a Toronto playwright, director, and filmmaker. *rihannaboi95* was first performed nightly from April 23 to 28, 2013, in an inner suburban Toronto bedroom and livestreamed to audience computers around the world. The play subsequently won the 2013 Dora Mavor Moore Award for Best New Play (TYA).

TRUTH IN ADVERSITY

THE CHILDREN'S REPUBLIC
BY HANNAH MOSCOVITCH

THE PLAY

The Children's Republic takes place in an orphanage in the Warsaw Ghetto during the Second World War. The ghetto was a walled area where Jewish people were forced to live. Essentially, it was a holding prison from which Jews were eventually sent to death camps. Against this darkest of backdrops, the play tells the story of a group of children who are living in an orphanage run by Dr. Janusz Korczak. Korczak was no ordinary orphanage director. He was a revolutionary champion of children and a signatory to the League of Nations's Declaration of the Rights of the Child. The contrast between the worst chapter in modern history and one of its most progressive voices is just one of the fascinating elements in this play.

THE SCENE

A locket has been stolen from a teacher. It is discovered being worn by a student, Mettye. Did she steal it? Dr. Korczak demands honesty in his school, and being honest means identifying the thief even if the thief is Mettye's friend, Israel. Korczak confronts the frightened boy and we discover his theft was an act of revenge for the teacher destroying a work of art. So Israel is tried, but so is the teacher! In what world can a group of students take a teacher to court? Perhaps in a world where justice is more important than privilege. And yet outside this "children's republic" six million Jews are being slaughtered.

THE CHARACTERS

Israel: A teenage boy.
Misha: A teenage girl.
Mettye: A teenage girl.
Sara: A teenage girl.
Janusz Korczak: A man in his sixties, director of the school and orphanage.
Stefa: A woman in her forties to fifties, Korczak's assistant.

CONNECTING WITH THE SCENE

What happens to children living in a country under invasion or occupation? How would their lives change? What happens to families during war?

Working in small groups, brainstorm and record on chart paper words, phrases, questions, titles of films and novels, examples, fragments of personal stories, and images that come to mind to describe the impact of war on children. Bring your chart paper to the centre of the room and tape the papers together to create and share a collective knowledge map with the other groups. Refer back to the map during the scene work and add thoughts and feelings and questions to the map as you work.

SCENE

STEFA sees the locket hanging around METTYE's neck. STEFA holds up the locket to show KORCZAK.

STEFA: *(to KORCZAK)* Look.

A beat of stillness.

KORCZAK: *(to METTYE, low)* Where did you get this?

Beat.

This locket: it's Madame Singer's locket.

STEFA: You stole it from her?

METTYE: No.

KORCZAK: You took it?

METTYE: No!

KORCZAK: This is Madame Singer's locket, Mettye.

METTYE: No!

STEFA: Yes it is.

METTYE: No, I was given it!

KORCZAK: By whom?

   Beat.

You took it.

METTYE: I didn't!

STEFA: *(a warning)* Mettye—

METTYE: I didn't!!!

STEFA: Mettye, you're lying.

METTYE: I'm not / lying!

SARA: *(low)* She's not lying.

   Beat.

(low) She's not.

   Transition.

   *KORCZAK and STEFA in KORCZAK's office. KORCZAK is rubbing his eyes. Then he stops.
   Then he starts rubbing them again.*

STEFA: Don't.

KORCZAK: What?

STEFA: *Don't. Rub. Them.*

KORCZAK gives her a look, but stops rubbing them. A tense beat of waiting. KORCZAK goes to rub his eyes again but then looks at STEFA and doesn't. STEFA can't resist:

STEFA: It's *always* these ones who are your favourites, these difficult–

KORCZAK: *(as if for the millionth time)* I don't have favourites–

STEFA: *You love them*, you love the little *criminals*; I don't know what it is, but I hope you're not planning to let this one off–

KORCZAK: Stefa.

STEFA: Well it's a serious thing to–

KORCZAK: *(under STEFA's line)* –Stefa–

STEFA: –lay the blame with another child–

KORCZAK: I know.

STEFA: Good, good. Fine. As long as you know it's very serious.

KORCZAK: I know.

STEFA: Fine–fine.

> *Beat.*

Fine.

> *ISRAEL appears in the doorway.*

ISRAEL: Doctor?

KORCZAK: Come in.

> *ISRAEL enters and stands before them, nervous. KORCZAK holds out the locket to him. ISRAEL eyes him, eyes the locket. Beat.*

Why did you take the locket?

Beat.

You took it—why?

STEFA clicks her tongue.

Why did you give it to Mettye? Did you hope she would take the blame?

ISRAEL: No.

KORCZAK: No? Why give it to her then—

STEFA: What else have you stolen?

ISRAEL: *(to STEFA)* Nothing.

STEFA clicks her tongue.

KORCZAK: Why, then? Why did you take it?

KORCZAK sighs. Rubs his eyes. Then stops himself.

You won't tell me?

STEFA: *(to KORCZAK)* He just took it.

KORCZAK: *(to ISRAEL)* Israel?

Beat. ISRAEL looks at him.

(to ISRAEL, low) Make at least one . . . catastrophic attempt.

Beat. ISRAEL looks away.

Look at me.

KORCZAK moves towards ISRAEL.

ISRAEL *flinches back, on reflex.* KORCZAK *gets hold of him.*

(frustrated) Look at me—I'm not—

Simultaneous text:

I'm not going to hit you.

ISRAEL: *(rushed, under his breath, hard to hear)* She tore up my . . .

KORCZAK: What? What did you say?

ISRAEL: *(low)* She tore up my . . .

KORCZAK: She tore up . . . what?

ISRAEL: *(low)* It was just a drawing.

KORCZAK: She tore up your drawing? Why?

ISRAEL: I don't know.

KORCZAK: What was the drawing of?

ISRAEL *shrugs.*

STEFA *clicks her tongue.*

ISRAEL: *(defiant, to* STEFA*)* Nothing.

STEFA: He's lying.

ISRAEL: No I'm not.

STEFA: *(to* KORCZAK*)* He's lying—

ISRAEL: I'm not *lying*!

ISRAEL *goes to attack* STEFA, *who recoils.* KORCZAK *gets hold of him before he reaches her.* KORCZAK *shakes him, holds him, and looks at him.*

ISRAEL: *(low)* I was trying to . . . ! I was trying to remember something.

STEFA *clicks her tongue.*

ISRAEL *looks at* STEFA, *twists out of* KORCZAK's *arms, turns, and walks out.*

KORCZAK: Israel! Israel! *(to* STEFA*)* Stefa . . . !

STEFA *clicks her tongue.*

Transition.

We're in the children's court. METTYE's *reading from a paper.* STEFA's *taking notes as the court clerk.*

METTYE: *(reading, looking down)* . . . The children's court's trying Madame Singer for tearing up Israel's drawing. The court sent a note to Madame Singer but she wouldn't come to court. *(to* MISHA*)* Uh. Misha?

MISHA *takes the stand.*

Did you see the drawing?

MISHA: I—yeah—I . . . yes.

METTYE: What was it of?

MISHA: There was a . . . man—he was in a blanket, and he was throwing up blood into a bucket. There was blood on the floor.

METTYE: Misha, step down. Israel?

METTYE *looks at* ISRAEL *and points at the dock.* MISHA *steps down as* ISRAEL *walks up.*

Who was in the drawing?

Beat.

Who was in the / drawing?

ISRAEL: *(low)* My father.

METTYE: Your father?

ISRAEL: *(nods slightly, then, low)* Yeah. I don't know.

STEFA: *(to ISRAEL, sharp)* Speak up.

ISRAEL: *(to STEFA)* Yeah.

METTYE: Step down.

   ISRAEL steps down.

(reading) The jury'll arrive at a verdict and write to Madame Singer. In the last session, the court tried Israel for stealing Madame Singer's locket. Israel?

   ISRAEL goes back across to the stand.

(reading) The court's found Israel guilty. The court's agreed to let the doctor sentence Israel.

KORCZAK: Thank you.

METTYE: *(referring to the paper)* That's all.

STEFA: *(to METTYE, to take the paper)* Good: here.

   METTYE hands the paper to STEFA, and the court files out. When it clears, METTYE sidles up to ISRAEL.

METTYE: *(casually, making conversation to get his attention)* You have lice.

   ISRAEL looks at her.

Just don't touch my face.

Beat. ISRAEL looks away.

You told me it was yours. You told me she gave it to you because it looks like you.

ISRAEL: *(low)* Yeah.

METTYE: Why'd you lie?

ISRAEL shrugs.

So I would be in trouble?

ISRAEL: Yeah.

METTYE: That's why?

Beat.

Why—why—

ISRAEL: I wanted to . . . give it to you.

METTYE: Why?

ISRAEL: To . . . *give it to you.*

METTYE: *Why.*

Beat. METTYE realizes why. Blushes.

Oh!!! You—you . . . !? *That's why*?!

ISRAEL: Yeah . . . ?

METTYE: You . . . gave me a stolen locket because you . . . *like me.*

ISRAEL: Yeah.

METTYE: You're a little stupid?

ISRAEL: Yeah?

METTYE: You . . . like me? That's nice. You . . . like me?

ISRAEL shrugs.

That's nice.

ISRAEL: Yeah?

DIGGING DEEPER INTO THE SCENE

Exploring Meaning

Notes on Fox and Rabbit Version One

Notes on Fox and Rabbit Version One

Using a game as an activity that relates to the subject matter of the scene or play can be very meaningful. This game will be used to help learners understand the meaning of rejection, inclusion, and difference. The game might be played at the beginning of the scene exploration to introduce themes or at any point during the work to help students experience and understand these ideas.

When introducing this game, ensure that there is plenty of room between the pairs who stand randomly around the room. Run through it first in slow motion to clarify the rules and to ensure that everyone has an equal chance to play.

Fox and Rabbit Version One

Find a partner. Stand facing your partner while holding hands. The space between you is called a "rabbit hole." The space around you is where the fox will chase the rabbit. Another pair will volunteer to be the fox and the rabbit.

The fox chases the rabbit. To escape the fox, the rabbit must run into a convenient "rabbit hole" before being tagged by the fox.

The person who faces the rabbit as she/he ducks under must grab the new partner's hands, and the previous partner becomes the new rabbit. If a rabbit is tagged, it becomes a fox and the roles are reversed.

Fox and Rabbit Version Two

In version two, the game changes so that any rabbit hole can remain open or be closed, preventing a place of safety for the rabbit.

This decision should happen organically in the moment as the rabbit approaches with no talking or signalling to the partner you're holding hands with.

Be prepared for a lot of noise as this is a fast-moving activity!

Notes on Fox and Rabbit Version Two

Allow the activity to continue for a little while so that students can experience this change.

Fox and Rabbit Discussion

As A Pair

How did you make the decision to close the rabbit hole as a rabbit approached?

Which of the two of you made the decision to shut the rabbit out?

Did you go along with the decision or try to change it?

When you were a part of a rabbit hole, how did it feel to close someone else out?

As the Rabbits

How did it feel to be closed out?

What similarities are there between this game and the situation in the scene or in the Warsaw Ghetto?

Circle Read

Circle Read Notes

Instead of breaking down into groups of five, you may want the whole class to read together in a circle.

On the second reading, start with a different student so that the readings differ from the first read-through.

After they have explored the text together in groups of five, have students choose their parts, or assign the roles yourself.

Read the scene silently alone.

Form a group of five and read together in a circle, reading the lines aloud, but not as the characters. One person begins reading a line and the person beside them reads the next line. Read through in this way twice.

Have each person in the group select a character to read as and read through the scene again. Change characters and repeat, paying attention to entrances and exits of the different characters.

Change characters again and read the scene standing and facing each other in two lines.

Change again and read through quickly, slowly, loudly, or softly whispering.

Spread out through the room and walk towards each other while reading your lines.

Change the order of the scene, beginning halfway through or at the end and work through each section, moving back to the first section of the scene.

Break into smaller groups of two or three in character and read through your particular sections. For example, you may wish to break into a group of three to read Stefa, Korczak, and Israel's section, or into a group of two to read Korczak and Stefa's dialogue.

Questions

What five things do you know for sure about the scene and characters?

What five unanswered questions do you have about the scene and characters? Is there anything about either that you wonder about?

Document your responses, rereading the scene if needed.

Share your questions with a partner, group, or the whole class, noting similarities and differences between the questions.

Building Authentic Characters and Relationships

Before the Orphanage

Before the Orphanage Notes

Students can share their stories in their groups or with the whole class or with a group of students all playing the same character.

This activity will help the students begin to build a backstory to deepen their understanding of the character.

In role as your character, imagine life before the orphanage.

Find, create, or mime an artifact that you brought with you from your life before the war and share the story of this artifact with your group.

In your story consider who gave it to you, why it is important to you, and what it tells us of your life then and now and in the future.

Overheard Conversations

Notes on Overheard Conversations

In this activity students are both participants and audience members as the scenes unfold for a minute or two. Students should be ready to pick up the scene as they may be called upon again.

Following the activity, ask the students to reflect on what they have learned about their characters and the situation. How will they take this into the rehearsal of the scene?

Notes on Writing in Role

This activity could deepen the work either at this point in the exploration of character or at the end to facilitate further reflection. Writing the notes will give the students an opportunity to articulate directly their intentions and motivations in the scene.

If there is time, students may wish to share the words they underlined in a group choral piece, or they could respond to the note in writing in their chosen role. See the Glossary on page 185 for choral speaking strategies.

In role as your character, imagine life in the orphanage. How would you feel in the morning? Would there be enough food at meals? What do you fear and hope for in this place? What do we know from the script about hygiene and living conditions in the orphanage? What do we know about the feelings of the staff?

Imagine the day after Israel's picture was torn up and the locket was stolen. Each group will choose a moment in that day and create an image (tableau) depicting life in the orphanage. Choose a moment from early in the morning, at a mealtime, during clean-up or chores, in the afternoon, evening, or at night.

Freeze in the image (tableau), and on a signal from the instructor, bring the scene to life for a few moments. Speak or whisper your inner thoughts or feelings about the orphanage, about the situation with Israel and the other children. At another signal, freeze again as the focus moves to another group. Try to create an authentic moment in the orphanage through both your physical position and your words.

Writing in Role

If you could send a note to another character in your scene, whom would you choose to send the note to? What would you want that character to know? Explain your actions or express your feelings in words that are unsaid in the script. Decide ahead of time who you will be writing to, ensuring each person will receive a note.

When you are done writing, exchange notes. Read the note given to you and circle the words that you are most moved by, that are the most important to you.

Share these words with the writer and explain why you chose them.

Corridor of Voices

Korczak is now faced with the task of sentencing Israel for theft. He has few resources and is responsible for many orphans. What if the other orphans begin stealing? What do you think would be a fair sentence?

Corridor of Voices Notes

What advice for sentencing will the students offer to Korczak? As he walks slowly down the corridor listening to each person, what advice will he hear and what decision will he make? Invite a student to play Israel and place him at the end of the line. Ask the student in role as Korczak to tell Israel his decision.

Sit quietly in your own space and think carefully about who you are in role. What have you experienced that has left you as an orphan with no family? Think about Korczak's difficult task of maintaining the orphanage amidst the dangers of the ghetto.

Imagine you have the opportunity to give Korczak advice to help him make his sentencing decision. You may choose to be one of the orphans, a staff member, Ms. Singer, or his own conscience.

Choose someone amongst you to stand in for Korczak, and as a group make two lines facing each other so there is a corridor between you.

Korczak will walk slowly down the corridor while each student in turn advises him. Listen carefully to the other voices, and, as Korczak passes, give him your advice.

Use the prompt: "I think you should sentence Israel to . . . *because* . . . "

You may also choose to use an alternate prompt if you feel sentencing is unjust: "I don't think you should sentence Israel . . . because . . . "

Create a Working Set

Notes on Creating a Working Set

In this activity students will begin to have those important discussions about character and context and will consider the variety of possibilities connected to both as they recreate the scene and place themselves on the set.

Create a space in the classroom as your working set. Consider what you need to create a space that speaks to us about where the characters are, the time of day, etc.

How will you create the orphans' world? Are they in a communal space in the orphanage or have they found a private place? Where is this private space? How will the audience know if it's private or not?

How will you create a space that can transition from one space to an entirely different one, changing from Korczak's office to the children's court?

With script in hand recreate the scene in your working set.

Work through the scene again, this time changing roles.

Artifacts

Notes on Artifacts

To prepare you might consider bringing in minimal items to make the scene come alive.

Students may also wish to bring in items that give meaning to their character and that give the suggestion of time and place.

It may be useful to talk about the clothing worn at the time (a lack of manufactured clothing, many handmade items, etc.).

The use of neutral shades by actors and in the set design will reinforce the shortage of materials and lack of access to food and clothes at the time.

Find or bring in props and/or costume pieces that will help you transform your character and the space.

Read through the scene again on your set with the necessary props and costume pieces.

Work through the scene while carefully following the stage directions.

Consider how you will make the transitions from one physical location to another in the scene.

Without special lighting, what techniques will you use to shift the focus? How will you bring the other performers on stage?

Rehearsing/Presenting

There are a variety of ways to rehearse and present a scene. Many of the above activities and strategies are rehearsal techniques, and at times we use presentation activities during the rehearsal process to further prepare for a performance.

Below is one performance example that you may wish to try for this scene, and you can find even more options by turning to Performance Possibilities on page 177. You can also come up with your own strategies for presenting your scene using these examples as maps. Discuss with your partner or group which presentation strategy works best for your chosen scene.

The transition in this scene from Korczak's office into the children's court is challenging. Create three groups. One group will rehearse or present the scene in Korczak's office, the second group will rehearse or present in the children's court, and the third will work on providing images and/or a soundscape to accompany the scene transitions to facilitate change of actors and set.

As the third group, decide what images, or tableaux, will provide a transition between the scenes. Make sure the images convey a clear, powerful message to the audience. For the soundscape, decide what atmosphere will link the scenes. Using found objects and your voices create/rehearse the atmosphere, considering variations of volume for maximum effect. You may wish to add one or two words at certain points in your images and/or soundscape. As a whole class, rehearse the scenes and transitions, then decide which transitions were the most powerful in your presentation.

Reflecting

Memory Circle

The children in Korczak's orphanage did not survive the war. They were sent to Treblinka, a death camp.

Imagine that many years after the war a memorial was created in the ghetto to remember the children, Korczak, and Stefa.

Consider how they might be remembered given what you know and imagine about their characters in the scene.

Standing in a circle and beginning with the statement "I remember," one by one share a memory of a character. You might share a line from the script: "I remember Stefa saying to Korczak, 'You love them, you love the little criminals.' "

Move into the circle and take a physical position to represent your memory of the character, holding it until the last person shares their memory and takes their own position in the circle. This will create the memorial statue and the words to be written on it.

As you come into the centre, take a shape to connect to another student in the image. Together you will create a final image to remember the children and their protectors. e.g. "I remember Korczak. He walked through the halls at night checking on the children."

NOTES TO THE ACTORS AND DIRECTORS

The playwright describes the children in this play as being traumatized. First, they are lost, or abandoned by their parents. Second, they are herded by the Nazis into a ghetto where food is scarce and death ever-present. How do you play a character that is traumatized? You don't. You play a character trying to be normal despite being traumatized. And what are the effects of trauma? This is something you will need to research!

Research will also be essential in answering two other questions. First, who was Janusz Korczak? He was a real person and you can be certain the playwright, Hannah Moscovitch, studied his character. The second question pertains to the Warsaw Ghetto. What were the conditions there? What was its citizens' relationship to the Germans? What was in store for their future? Were they aware of the death camps?

And finally, a note to the director: knowing that we are in the Warsaw Ghetto is an essential part of the story. How will you make this clear to the audience?

PLAYWRIGHT AND PRODUCTIONS

A graduate of the National Theatre School of Canada, Hannah Moscovitch is one of the finest voices in Canadian theatre. She is particularly interested in stories about adolescence. If you are interested in reading another of her plays, try *In This World*. *The Children's Republic* premiered in Ottawa at the Great Canadian Theatre Company in 2009 and was subsequently remounted in Toronto at the Tarragon Theatre in 2011.

Related Resources

Friends of Simon Wiesenthal Center for Holocaust Studies is a non-profit human rights organization committed to countering racism and anti-Semitism, and to promoting the principles of tolerance, social justice, and Canadian democratic values through advocacy and education: www.friendsofsimonwiesenthalcenter.com

The Holocaust Explained (suitable for ages fourteen and up): www.theholocaustexplained.org

Information and a history of Janusz Korczak and the Warsaw Ghetto from the Jewish Virtual Library: www.jewishvirtuallibrary.org/jsource/biography/Korczak.html

A catalogue of paintings by Felix Nussbaum, a German Jewish painter who depicted his life during the Holocaust in his art. He was ultimately killed in Auschwitz: www.felix-nussbaum.de/werkverzeichnis/archiv.php?lang=en&

912 Days of the Warsaw Ghetto, a short documentary on life in Warsaw during the war: www.youtube.com/watch?v=OfbWsjeePKg

The Janusz Korczak Association of Canada: www.januszkorczak.ca

Facing History and Ourselves, an organization that provides ideas, methods, and tools that support the practical needs, and the spirits, of educators worldwide who share the goal of creating a better, more informed, and more thoughtful society: www.facinghistory.org

Related Plays

Hana's Suitcase by Emil Sher, adapted from the story by Karen Levine

Such Creatures by Judith Thompson

Corpus by Darrah Teitel

THE UNPLUGGING
BY YVETTE NOLAN

THE PLAY

The Unplugging takes place in a future with no electricity, which means no communication, transportation, or refrigeration. Food is scarce. People are forced to make brutal decisions. Elena and Bern are two older women banished from their community for being "unproductive." Expected to die in the harsh winter weather, they rediscover the hunting and survival skills of their grandparents and prosper. Their fragile peace is threatened, however, by the appearance of a desperate young man who needs to be accepted by these two cautious women to survive.

THE SCENES

In the first scene, Bern, alert to her environment, becomes aware of Seamus and calls him out. She has a knife but she wonders aloud if she has the will to kill. In this desperate new world where everything has changed, is there a new morality? Seamus seems friendly enough but he's vague about his recent past. Where did he come from? Being friendly is not enough. Being friendly may be an act before the attack. Seamus is also assessing the situation. We know from reading the whole play that he has been sent from the community who banished Bern and Elena to see if they have survived and, if they have, to steal whatever would be useful for the community's survival. But as the scene progresses, Bern becomes more than a name, more than a target. And besides . . . she has that knife.

In the second scene, Bern has decided that Seamus is safe, perhaps even useful and desirable. Yet she has kept her contact with the outsider a secret from Elena, with whom she has an intimate and trusting friendship. In this scene, Bern tries to persuade Elena to allow Seamus to enter their private place, which forces her to admit to her lie.

THE CHARACTERS

Bern: a woman who has been banished from her community.
Elena: a woman who has been banished from her community.
Seamus: a young man, travelling through the forest near where Bern and Elena live.

CONNECTING WITH THE SCENES

Notes on Connecting With the Scenes

There are two scenes in this study that are connected through the character of Bern and follow closely one after the other in the play. They both demonstrate the impact of banishment on the characters. The class could be divided in two, with each half tackling one scene, or the whole class could work on one scene at a time. The scenes do stand on their own. The teaching and learning strategies for this piece offer the students an opportunity to work with the text and the scenes in their entirety as though they had been cast in the play.

The title of this play is *The Unplugging*. What thoughts and/or images come to mind when you think of an "unplugging"? Consider how your life would be changed if you had to "unplug" all power. Consider how the world would be changed if it became "unplugged." Share your thoughts with a partner or with the class.

Scene One

> BERN *is out foraging, near the monk's place. She stops a couple of times, sensing something. Then continues. Then stops.*

BERN: hello? Is there someone there?

> *She takes out a knife.*

come out.

> SEAMUS *enters, hands held apart. He is young enough, handsome, a bit hungry looking.*

SEAMUS: Hi.

> *Beat.*

BERN: Hi?

SEAMUS: yeah, hi. We used to say it all the time to people when we met them.

BERN: Ha.

SEAMUS: no, hi.

> *Beat.*

do you think—you could—

> *He motions to the knife.*

—it's not very welcoming—

BERN: maybe I'm not very welcoming

SEAMUS: tough luck for me, then

BERN considers him for a moment. Puts the knife away.

thank you.

BERN shrugs.

glad you trust me

BERN: I don't

SEAMUS: but

BERN: that's about me, not you. You may still be a rapist, or a murderer, you may still want to harm me. And if you do, if you try, I will fight you, but you look kinda hungry and not very strong, and I am not hungry and I am strong. So.

SEAMUS: So?

BERN: So. I don't want to be the kind of person who can kill someone. And if I have a knife, then I am choosing to use the knife, and that means I have to be ready to kill you. I don't think I am that person.

SEAMUS: wow. Did you just think all that right now?

BERN laughs.

what?

BERN: so what are you doing here?

SEAMUS: just found myself here.

BERN: where did you come from?

SEAMUS points vaguely.

really. You have been just wandering since the unplugging.

SEAMUS: the unplugging? That's what you call it? An apocalypse destroys half the world, and you call it the unplugging?

BERN shrugs.

BERN: I used to think of it as the earth waking and shaking like some great dog, and all the machines and wires being shaken off like so many fleas. The earthquakes in Haiti and Japan, the disappearance of the Maldives . . . But that was really negative. The unplugging is more—benign.

SEAMUS: benign?

BERN: yeah. Like—mild. Harmless, kind of.

SEAMUS: benign.

BERN: how old are you?

SEAMUS: old enough

BERN: what are you doing here?

SEAMUS: free country

BERN laughs again.

why do you keep laughing at me?

BERN: you say funny things

SEAMUS: I don't think I do

BERN: what are you doing here?

SEAMUS: same as you, probably. Looking for stuff. Trying to stay alive.

BERN: where'd you come from? Yeah, yeah, I know.

She motions vaguely as he did before.

But it's been seven or eight moons since the unplugging. You haven't been wandering since then. You've been somewhere; you've been part of some community. And now you are not. How come?

Scene Two

> BERN *is doing housework.* ELENA *bursts through the door carrying the hatchet. She gets the rifle, starts to load it.*

BERN: Elena, what—?

ELENA: they've found us

BERN: who's found us? Wait, Elena—

ELENA: not now, Bernadette.

> BERNADETTE *grabs the rifle barrel.* ELENA *still holds the stock.*

BERN: what—are—you—doing?

ELENA: there's a man out there. Watching us.

BERN: a man?

ELENA: they've sent someone, Bernadette. They tracked us, and they've sent someone—

BERN: why would they do that, Elena?

ELENA: to take what we have. Let go.

BERN: you're not going to shoot him

ELENA: I am going to try.

BERN: he's hardly a man, Elena. Not much more than a boy.

ELENA stops. Beat. Beat.

BERN: I met him. Yesterday. Up near the monk's place.

ELENA: you—*met*—him?

BERN: yeah, I was on my way back from the creek and I could feel that I was being watched. So I called him out.

ELENA: you met him yesterday? And you didn't tell me?

BERN: I'm sorry, Elena. I was trying to figure out how to—tell you.

ELENA is silent.

I was afraid. Of this. That you would take a gun to him.

ELENA: you met him yesterday.

BERN: I'm sorry.

Beat.

Elena, can we invite him in?

ELENA: no.

BERN: no?

ELENA: absolutely not.

BERN: I don't get a say in this?

ELENA: how about, I don't get a say in this. You go off and meet some man, you don't tell me, now you want to bring him into our house.

BERN: sorry, sorry, sorry, how many times can I say it? I'm sorry. Elena, it's cold out there; he is hungry. He's young, and kinda dumb.

ELENA: Send him back to them. Tell them no.

BERN: They banished him.

    Beat.

ELENA: Sure they did.

BERN: That's what he says.

ELENA: Don't believe him, Bernadette. He's a man.

BERN: oh my god

ELENA: How long did you two stand around chatting? Or was it more than chatting?

BERN: It was more like talking, Elena. Not too long. Long enough. He's staying in the monk's place.

ELENA: nooooo

BERN: no it's okay. I checked. He is being respectful. Showed him how to make a proper fire.

ELENA: you were in the monk's place with him

BERN: He has news, Elena, lots of news.

DIGGING DEEPER INTO THE SCENES

Exploring Meaning

Text Play

Read the scenes silently to yourself.

Read the scenes aloud in a group of three.

Change roles and read again so that everyone has an opportunity to read each character.

Read the scenes sitting back to back, standing close to each other, and then farther away.

Read the scenes while changing the volume of your voice, from whispering to shouting.

Read the scenes quickly with a sense of urgency.

Read the scenes with Elena angry and loud, and Seamus and Bern calm and quiet.

Read the scenes with Seamus and Bern angry and loud, and Elena quiet and calm.

Continue to experiment with reading all three parts.

Notes on Text Play

Encourage the students to play with the text, keeping an open mind around interpretation.

Reassure the students not to feel restricted by gender. A female can play Seamus and a male can play Bern or Elena.

Questions

What five things do you know for sure about the scene and characters?

What five unanswered questions do you have?

What do you wonder about?

Document your responses, rereading the scene if needed.

Share with your partners, another group, or the whole class, noting similarities and differences between the questions.

Building Authentic Characters and Relationships

Interpreting Stage Directions

Bern and Seamus meet while foraging, an act of searching or rummaging on the land for food, plants, edible grasses, etc.

Continue the action of foraging through the entire first scene. This might mean you hardly ever look at the other character because you are foraging to access hidden supplies. Or there might be moments where you are looking at the other character though they are not looking at you.

Were there any moments where it felt right to be foraging?

At what moments did the text force you to stop and look at your partner?

How will you integrate this new learning into the scene?

Now play the scene while selectively incorporating the foraging as one of the actions of the characters.

Consider another action your character might engage in at another part of the scene. Repeat the scene including both actions.

The student playing Elena can act as director for this activity. Simply observe to learn more, and participate in the discussion after the activity. What did you learn about the characters?

Meeting

"SEAMUS enters, hands held apart. He is young enough, handsome, a bit hungry looking."

Try the physical gesture "hands held apart" in a variety of ways. What might that look like, and what might it mean?

How would it look with the direction, "hands in pockets" or "hands at his sides"? Try the different ways to observe the different attitudes.

Discuss with your partners what "young enough" means.

What personal choices might you make to communicate "a bit hungry looking"? Consider inside thoughts and feelings, and outside signifiers, such as facial hair, makeup, clothing choices, etc.

Notes on Interpreting Stage Directions

Students will have fun reading through the script and foraging at the same time. Have them speed up or slow down to encourage meaningful revisiting of the script.

Meeting Notes

Sometimes it can be important to explore stage directions with students, but it's also important to remember that sometimes stage directions can restrict the exploration.

In this strategy encourage students to interpret the stage directions to better understand the playwright's intentions in their use.

Look at the stage directions for scene two, particularly the direction "Elena stops. Beat. Beat." Discuss with your partners what that means. How long would that be? What would they be doing in that moment?

Shifting Power

Play through the scenes.

Notes on Shifting Power

Discuss the notion of power and how it is identified and communicated. Encourage students to read the text carefully, noting if the power is exhibited through the words, the actions, or the use of props and what is not said but felt or thought.

Each time that you feel that the power has shifted for your character, either received or relinquished, freeze for a moment and then continue.

Negotiate with your partner and agree on two moments where the power shifts from character to character in the scene.

Make a note of these moments.

While the students are playing scene one, the students playing Elena can observe and comment on their choices. The character playing Seamus can do the same when observing scene two.

Still Image

Create three contrasting images, one where Bern has the power, one where Seamus has the power, and one where Elena has the power (in the second scene).

Still Image Notes

Deconstruct one or two of the images with the students, asking them what they see, what they think they see, and how it makes them feel about the characters. Images can be presented simultaneously, in a carousel, or by dividing the group in half with one half sharing and the other half observing.

As you build these images consider distance between characters. How close might you be to a stranger, or a friend with a rifle?

Think about the physicality or positioning of your character and how that conveys how you are feeling. Would you make eye contact, or look away? Where would you be looking?

Add a slow-motion transition so that the three images are seamlessly connected.

Share this work with another group or with the whole class.

Banishment

Elena and Bern have been banished from the community that exists after the unplugging. It is uncertain why the man outside, Seamus, is on his own.

Decide with your partners why the women were banished and are on their own.

Create a still image to represent this banishment and give the image a title.

Create a second still image to represent why Seamus is now outside on his own. Share the images and titles with another group or with the whole class.

Discuss how creating this backstory will help you better understand the characters and play the scene.

Create a Working Set

The scene takes place in two separate places. How will your set accommodate the two scenes?

What would be needed to convey this? What props do they need in the scenes? How will you create the "outdoors"?

Using the same space, utilize the available furniture and props to create the cottage.

How and where will you establish the window in the room?

What props or objects will you use to give the audience the sense of the gun?

Make sure to establish entrances and exits.

Consider how you will make the transitions from scene to scene.

Notes on Creating a Working Set

Discuss with the students something they could use to signify the weapons if you are working in an environment where replica weapons are not permitted. Encourage the students to find imaginative ways to solve the problem.

Rehearsing/Presenting

You may want to present one or both of the scenes, or even present a section of each scene with the transition from one to the other so all have an opportunity to present.

Reflecting

Improvisation

Notes on Improvisation

Encourage students to reveal in role thoughts and feelings that are not being articulated in the script (the subtext). This work will bring out a variety of perspectives.

Invite the listeners to ask questions that will challenge the characters to develop new understandings.

In this improvisation, all of the Berns will describe or retell the encounter with Seamus to the Elenas, who will both listen to the story and ask questions for more information.

Following the improvisation, Seamus will retell his version of the story to a couple of friends from his previous community.

The students playing Bern and Elena will take on the role of the friends who will both listen to the story and ask questions for information.

Finding the Truth

Notes on Finding the Truth

Discuss universal themes with the students, asking them what the scene is really about, what there is to learn about our world.

Following the presentations, identify these truths and discuss how the scenes communicated these themes.

These scenes take place in the future when the world became unplugged and changed forever, and yet it is about many other ideas and truths.

Discuss with your group or with the whole class what you think the scenes are about, the universal truth they are reflecting.

Improvise an analogous scene set in today's world that reveals the same theme.

Present the scenes to the class.

NOTES TO THE ACTORS AND DIRECTORS

In *The Children's Republic* the danger was outside the orphanage. In this scene, the danger is onstage as Bern and Seamus confront each other. In a situation where words can be lies, body language is crucial. Play the scene once with maximum suspicion and fear. Use more movement and gesture than feels natural. Now play it again and try to hide those markers. Despite the instinct to attack or run away, try and appear relaxed, even as you are alert and suspicious.

What a character says onstage is only a part of what is interesting about theatre. What the character doesn't say is often more interesting. It forces us, the audience, to pay attention to movement, tonal qualities, and hidden emotions. In the second scene, what is Bern hiding? What is Elena hiding?

PLAYWRIGHT AND PRODUCTIONS

Yvette Nolan is a First Nations playwright, dramaturg, and director. She is a former artistic director of Native Earth Performing Arts. *The Unplugging* was first produced by the Arts Club Theatre in Vancouver in 2009 and is inspired by the novel *Two Old Women* by Velma Wallis.

READING AND RESEARCHING

Related Resources

Stories about unplugging in everyday life: www.huffingtonpost.ca/news/unplugging/

A list of nineteen signs that indicate you need to unplug from your smartphone: www.huffingtonpost.com/2013/11/23/signs-you-need-to-unplug_n_4268822.html

This new story about a UN environmental report points towards the reality that we could face our own unplugging in the future: www.arstechnica.com/uncategorized/2007/10/new-un-environmental-report-paints-a-very-bleak-future-for-humanity/

The Assembly of First Nations website on honouring and saving the earth: www.afn.ca/index.php/en/honoring-earth

Related Plays

Norah's Ark by Jasmine Dubé, translated by Linda Gaboriau

The Shunning by Patrick Friesen

OIL AND WATER
BY ROBERT CHAFE

THE PLAY

Oil and Water's inspiration comes from the life of Lanier Phillips, a celebrated African American civil rights activist. The play moves back and forth between two important moments in Lanier's life. The first takes place in 1942 when he was a sailor aboard the USS *Truxton*, a navy ship carrying over a hundred soldiers. The ship ran aground off the coast of Newfoundland, killing most of its men. Lanier was the sole African American survivor and the first black man to be seen by the residents of St. Lawrence, Newfoundland. The play dramatically recreates the moments when Lanier, left on the sinking ship by his white crew mates, swims to shore, and is rescued and cared for by local residents. Lanier claimed this experience of goodness and humanity, in contrast to the racism of his homeland, changed his life and made him a supporter of Martin Luther King Jr. and the civil rights movement. The second part of his story, which in the play occurs first, takes place in the 1960s. Lanier is now the father of a thirteen-year-old girl who is experiencing the forced integration of American schools. A tale of two cultures and two times, *Oil and Water* is a vision for a just and tolerant society.

THE SCENES

In the scenes we have chosen, we first see Lanier in the 1960s arguing with his daughter Vonzia. Vonzia is refusing to go to her new school in an all-white neighbourhood. Lanier is in favour of the integration of the school system and insists Vonzia "get on the bus." Check out the websites at the end of this scene for more information on the desegregation of the school system in the United Sates and the civil rights movement.

The second part takes place earlier, in 1942, on the deck of the USS *Truxton*. It is night and a winter storm is raging. A young Lanier (referred to in military fashion by his last name—Phillips) argues with Bergeron, a white sailor, for a place in the lifeboat.

THE CHARACTERS

Lanier: Fifty years old, black. Calm, poised, holds a strength unexplained except by his story.

Vonzia: Thirteen years old, black. Lanier's daughter, fiery, still growing up.

Phillips: Eighteen years old, black. Lanier earlier in his life. Young, idealistic, angry, and very smart. An American naval mess* attendant.

Bergeron: Twenty-four years old, white. Gutsy, congenial. An American naval seaman.

Langston: Twenty-one years old, black. An American naval mess attendant.

CONNECTING WITH THE SCENES

Notes on Connecting With the Scenes

There are two scenes in this study connected through the character of Lanier Phillips. They follow closely one after the other in the play and demonstrate the impact of racism in two different eras. The class could be divided in two, with each half tackling one scene, or the whole class could work on one scene at a time. The scenes do stand on their own. The following teaching and learning strategies offer the students an opportunity to work with the text and the scenes as an ensemble cast. The play may be performed by an ensemble cast with all of the characters on stage all of the time.

Think about an argument you have had with a parent or an adult over something that you felt very strongly about.

Find a partner and explore the first situation, taking the role of yourself first, and then taking the role of your parent with your partner taking the opposite role.

This time explore your partner's situation in the same way as before.

What understandings were you able to come to when exploring the other's point of view?

In what ways was the argument important at the time?

After playing both roles, what would you now do to attempt to resolve the conflict?

What does the title Oil and Water convey and how will it add to your scene work?

* Where military personnel eat.

Scene One

VONZIA: I ain't going!

LANIER: Vonzia, that bus a coming.

VONZIA: Let it come.

LANIER: Put your coat on, come on.

VONZIA: I ain't going back, I said.

LANIER: And how you figure that?

VONZIA: I'm gonna home-school.

LANIER: That right?

VONZIA: Good enough for half a class of white girls, good enough for me.

LANIER: Put your coat on, no fooling now.

VONZIA: They all staying home, leaving the cold and the cops for us, tell me how that's fair.

LANIER: I know fair and not fair, and I know you are getting on that bus.

VONZIA: You don't even know.

LANIER: I believe I do.

VONZIA: You read the paper this morning and tell me what you know.

LANIER: What's the paper going to tell me about you getting on that bus?

VONZIA: Tell you few reasons why I'm not. Tell you about a boy from Roxbury.

LANIER: Tell me what?

VONZIA: His knife and his temper.

LANIER: What boy?

VONZIA: A high-school boy. He getting it good like the rest of us, only he see fit to fight back. Take that knife of his to the cause of his grief, some white fella in his class down in Southie. They come face to face about it, and this boy from Roxbury, they say he–

LANIER: This true?

VONZIA: I'm a liar now? Everyone talking about it on the bus home yesterday.

LANIER: Vonzia–

VONZIA: Buy yourself a paper, you don't believe me! I'm sure it in there. Black boy stab a white fella, they didn't go and miss that.

LANIER: Why you not tell me this before?

VONZIA: I try to and you not listen! Didn't I tell you about the police and the teachers, it all the same!

LANIER: A boy got stabbed.

VONZIA: Figure you'd read it for yourself, hoping as much.

LANIER: That white boy, he gonna be all right?

VONZIA: I don't know, buy yourself a paper! You don't believe me about them cops down there, and them empty classroom seats. And them folks on the street, folks on the street, Daddy, morning and afternoon, how they stand and stare. Just like they never even set eyes on a bus before, can't believe what it is they're seeing. I know what they looking at; I know good and well.

LANIER: All right, baby, just calm down.

VONZIA: It gotta be a fight all the time. Yesterday it that boy from Roxbury, who it gonna be today?

LANIER: Not you.

VONZIA: It gotta be a fight, all the time a fight.

LANIER: It was a fight that got won that you even get to go to school at all, you see that.

VONZIA: I ain't going.

LANIER: Vonzia—

VONZIA: Them papers, they print what happened, yeah that the full story there for sure. A fella stab some white boy. And them papers gonna say what? Poor guy done nothing at all to deserve it. Except what I see with my eyes every day, what they done do to that boy from Roxbury, to us, to me, Daddy, what they done, I say good for him.

LANIER: Vonzia, enough.

VONZIA: That's what I say. Good for him that done it. Good for that white boy for getting it, for deserving what he got.

LANIER: I don't want to hear you saying such, you hear me?

VONZIA: Tell me you wouldn't do the same.

LANIER: Vonzia—

VONZIA: They a boot on your face and you wouldn't fight back?

LANIER: Yes, I would, and I have, baby, but not like—

VONZIA: You wouldn't fight for yourself and you in the navy.

LANIER: You don't know everything.

VONZIA: No I don't. And whose fault is that? Tell me nothing, that old picture dug out to stare at.*

---

* This is an old photo that Lanier keeps looking at. It is a picture of himself and the Newfoundland family who rescued him and cared for him after the shipwreck.

LANIER: Vonzia.

VONZIA: Tell me nothing, about it or the navy. Tell me nothing and do nothing because what? Because you afraid.

LANIER: You don't know everything!

A silence as VONZIA stares at him, startled. He immediately regrets his frustration. He moves towards her.

Baby. I'm sorry.

She backs away from him. A long silence as she slowly puts on her coat. He watches her.

You wearing it, you may as well button it up.

VONZIA: That bus too warm most days, driver let us put the windows down.

LANIER: Just think now, how lucky you are. It pick you up practically at our front door. It drop you at the new school directly.

She doesn't look at him. He goes to her, holds her by her shoulders, looks her in the eyes.

This a good school, a better school. And you given the chance, the choice to go there, baby. You been given that. Choice, it's a rare and precious thing in this world. Best make good use of it when we can.

She backs away from him.

VONZIA: I gotta go. Got me a warm bus ride across town.

She leaves. He stares after her.

Scene Two

LANGSTON chases PHILLIPS, moving over the icy wave-washed deck. All is panic.

LANGSTON: Phillips? Phillips? Where you going? You going the wrong way.

PHILLIPS: We run aground and still I feel her slipping under my feet. Oh Jesus. Feel that?

LANGSTON: They say to head back inside, they told us that, come on now.

PHILLIPS: They setting down boats off the fore'ard. Look, see for yourself.

LANGSTON: I can see fine.

PHILLIPS: Get us a seat on one of them to shore, come on.

LANGSTON: You heard what they told us. You know where it's cold like this, don't you?

PHILLIPS: We in the navy, registered, serving. We all standing shoulder to shoulder, and they setting boats down.

LANGSTON: They come and get us that's left, the navy, they will, they all say so.

PHILLIPS: I'm not going back down inside.

LANGSTON: Navy come and get us.

PHILLIPS: There's nothing to that. Bergeron!

LANGSTON: There's nothing waiting for us two on that shore. That's the truth. This here Iceland.

PHILLIPS: Bergeron!

BERGERON: Told you to go down and bring up blankets.

PHILLIPS: We itching to get to shore, see ourselves some space left.

BERGERON: Langston, every stitch of clothes you got. You hear me? Every stitch, you go put them on layer by layer.

LANGSTON: Yes, sir.

BERGERON: Don't dally now, water coming in fast below.

PHILLIPS: Don't we know.

LANGSTON: Come on, Phillips.

PHILLIPS: Room in that boat, room for ten men and it about to push off with but two.

BERGERON: Your math is faulty, that boat is full.

PHILLIPS: I can count to two.

BERGERON: That boat is full.

PHILLIPS: Enough room for you.

BERGERON: Step back, son.

PHILLIPS: I ain't your son. This ship a sinking.

> PHILLIPS *tries to get around him.* BERGERON *steps in front.*

BERGERON: You're not hearing me.

PHILLIPS: Get your hands off me!

LANGSTON: Come on, Phillips. Come on.

PHILLIPS: Leaving men to claw at ice!

BERGERON: Call off your dog, Langston.

PHILLIPS: A dog have a better shot at getting taken to shore!

BERGERON: And no man here think twice to put it down!

A standoff.

There is nothing I can do for you.

LANGSTON: Phillips, they all looking. Come on now, in case they throw you in theyself.

PHILLIPS takes a step back, his eyes still locked with BERGERON's. BERGERON goes. The men watch him.

PHILLIPS: His hands on me, pushing back to the deck of a sinking ship.

LANGSTON: Come on, we go in as they say. Phillips, you bloody fool, it warmer, them waves gonna sweep you right off.

PHILLIPS stands, watches the boat launch.

PHILLIPS: He get himself a spot in that full boat.

LANGSTON: Stubborn son of a bitch you is. Get yourself killed, you blame yourself.

PHILLIPS looks towards shore.

PHILLIPS: And we so close to shore. Look at it.

LANGSTON: Phillips!

LANGSTON shakes his head, bolts away, leaving PHILLIPS. PHILLIPS stares at the shore, a thought rolling in his head.

Exploring Meaning

Text Play

Read the scenes silently to yourself.

Read aloud in a group of five.

Switch roles and read again until each person in the group has read all the roles.

Standing and facing each other, read the scene again. Read the scenes sitting back to back in a circle.

Read the scenes with a large space between you, having to shout as if you were in a storm.

Negotiate the distance between your characters as you read the scenes.

Now try playing with the text, using emotions and feelings that are authentic to the characters' words.

Read the scenes with the characters in a straight line. The characters from scene one step forward and read the scene while the characters from scene two observe and respond with gestures and expression in silence. Repeat with the characters from scene two stepping forward.

How do these strategies of playing with text help you to understand the scenes?

Share your understandings with another group or with the whole class.

Notes on Text Play

Ensure all students in the group have an opportunity to play all roles during this activity.

Choose a variety of ways to unpack the text of the scenes so that students have opportunities to explore and reread the script.

Encourage students to concentrate on what is important to focus on while they are reading.

Students may choose ways to unpack the scenes that most suit the context, but it is always important to prepare a number of different ways to explore the text beforehand.

Only after significant exploration, invite the students to make a choice of which character to play.

Questions

How do these strategies of playing with text help you to understand the scenes?

In what way did physical contact with your partners affect character-ization? Was any one role more difficult than another to feel physical contact?

Share your understanding with another group or with the whole class.

What are five things you know for sure about the scenes and characters?

Think of five unanswered questions you have about the scenes and characters.

Is there anything about the scenes or characters you wonder about?

Document your responses, rereading the scenes if needed.

Share with your group or with the whole class, noting similarities and differences between the questions.

Building Authentic Characters and Relationships

Role On the Wall

Role on the Wall Notes

Ensure there is an ensemble group for each character. With a very small class one group could do two characters.

Ask the students to work collectively on the outlines in their groups, view the other groups' work, and then have them share the images with the rest of the class.

What is each character concerned with in these moments and in their lives? What have you learned about the characters on the outside from the two scenes? Do you know their ages, occupations, actions, connections?

In small ensemble groups create life-size outlines of one of the character from either scene on large sheets of paper or on a chalkboard.

Document everything you know about the characters' relationships to each other in the space between the characters in a different colour.

Working with different colours makes the learning explicit and assists in building a full vision of the character.

Groups of five students could also create all of the characters.

Document everything you think you know about them on the inside—their feelings, their fears, their hopes, and their values—in yet another colour.

What do you want to know, or have questions about for each character? What do you wonder about? Place these in a fourth colour around the perimeter of each outline.

As an ensemble group, move around to each of the other outlines, noting similarities and differences for each character and adding further questions or comments to clarify your understanding of that character.

Return to your outlines and share what you know about the character with another ensemble group or with the whole class.

Still Image Notes

Encourage the students to recreate the moment truthfully, ensuring it is from Vonzia's perspective and not based on assumptions.

Still Image

Working in your ensemble group, create a still image depicting a scene that Vonzia has experienced and is attempting to share with Lanier. This could be the bus ride, the bus's arrival at the school, or waiting at the bus stop.

Portray this moment from Vonzia's perspective, using your body, facial expressions, and physical placement.

Carousel Share Notes

Guide the students to view all of the images in a carousel, moving seamlessly from one to the other.

Deconstruct a couple of the images to closely examine Vonzia's perspective. This will also encourage discussion of the themes and background of the scene.

Tap the Vonzias in the image and ask them to share in role what they are feeling in this moment.

Carousel Share

As Vonzia in your ensemble group, be prepared to share your inner feelings in role if tapped on the shoulder, but remain frozen in the image.

Look carefully at the still images the other groups have created. What do you see that is clear? What is unclear?

Which facial expressions, body language, physical gestures, or distance between characters tell you how Vonzia is being received? What do you see about Vonzia that tells you how she is feeling?

With your group or as a whole class, discuss how physical proximity, body language, gestures, and facial expressions can add to the meaning of the scenes.

How will this exploration inform your representation of characters that are unfairly treated or experience racism or other forms of prejudice? How can you take this understanding into the scene?

Now I Get It!

Read through the scenes again and this time freeze the moment when you feel, in role, that you have a new understanding of the situation or of the relationship. Explain to your ensemble group your new understanding and continue reading.

How will your characterization change to reflect this moment?

One Word Line

In your ensemble try playing the scenes again with added physicality, but this time you can use only one word to extract the authentic meaning of your line, indicating what your character is showing on the *outside*.

Repeat, but this time the extracted word will reflect what the character is feeling on the *inside*.

How difficult was it to find the right word to reflect the authentic meaning of your line? How did this exercise inform your work?

Create a Working Set

With minimal furniture and props, create a working set for the scenes. Make a list of props that are mentioned in the scenes and collect them. Consider time and place when finding props and making costume choices.

Have the students find creative ways to develop the illusion of the storm and ship.

They will also need to find creative solutions for changing the set over quickly.

Rehearse the scenes in the set using the props. The set has to be easily struck or changed to quickly move into the second scene, which needs to feature both a boat and a storm.

Select props and costume pieces to help make the transition. You might want to also consider sound effects.

Remember, all of the actors remain on stage for both scenes. Where will your character be on the set? What will you be doing and how will you be responding when not speaking?

Although you will be responding when not speaking, be thoughtful of where the focus is at that moment.

Rehearsing/Presenting

This is an opportunity to share two scenes together as an ensemble. It will be interesting for the audience to see how you meet the challenge of making the transitions and working with the entire cast on stage throughout the scenes.

Reflecting

Notes on Another Perspective

Encourage the students to be authentic as they role-play, asking them to be thoughtful as they step into role as the wife or mother. This writing gives the students an opportunity to reflect on the scenes with a new perspective.

Another Perspective

We do not meet Lanier's wife—Vonzia's mother—in these scenes. Imagine how she would respond to these scenes and share your interpretation in a monologue that could appear at some point in one of the scenes. You could also write two or three entries in a blog that covers the time frame of the two scenes. Share an excerpt of your writing with your ensemble group.

Playwriting

Oil and Water is based on a true encounter in a real person's life. What have you learned about this person and his life through these scenes? How did the playwright use theatrical techniques to engage you in his life?

Think of encounters, situations, and real people today who you might want to write about in a play. Why do you think a play is a powerful way to tell someone's story? How is it different than a movie or biography?

Think about a real person and with a partner create an outline of the first scene of a play that tells this person's story. If you are interested in developing this further, write the first scene and share it with the class.

NOTES TO THE ACTORS AND DIRECTORS

To inhabit Vonzia and Lanier fully, you need to know as much as possible about the world they live in and the injustices they are experiencing. We know it has to do with racial prejudice against African Americans in the 1960s, but what does Vonzia's reference to "home-schooling" mean? What about "the cold and the cops"? The references to "Southie" and "Roxbury" might be a clue to where this scene takes place. Are these rich neighbourhoods, or poor? There is a reference to a white boy being stabbed. Is that a true story? Vonzia refers to newspapers, so that might be a good place to start, as they can convey emotion. What is Vonzia's attitude towards newspapers? Is it the same as Lanier's? Lanier is very insistent that Vonzia go to school. Why is it so important to him? Why is it such a big "opportunity" for his daughter?

The strategies in Text Play and Building Authentic Characters and Relationships will help you to find answers to some of these questions, to find understanding in the lines, and to internalize the emotional journey of the characters. Clearly the first scene has a conflict that leads to Lanier losing his temper. However, playing anger or frustration can become boring quickly if there is no variety. How does the argument build? What is the struggle the characters are having within themselves? For example, Lanier is clearly struggling to be patient but what is Vonzia's struggle? At the end of the scene, Vonzia decides to get on the bus. What makes her change her mind? How will you play this?

In the second scene the action suddenly changes from a domestic setting to the icy deck of a ship in a storm. The character of Phillips is Lanier at the age of eighteen. As you can see from the text, the two scenes flow from one to the other without a break or pause. Here is a wonderful challenge for your theatrical imagination! How will you portray the ship? The storm? Will you incorporate sound and or music? How will the actor play Lanier as a young man? There is clearly a power imbalance between Bergeron on one side and Phillips and Langston on the other. Langston appears to accept this imbalance. Why? Phillips doesn't. Why? How did Bergeron get this power? One clue to staging this scene, and emphasizing the power imbalance, might be the number of characters on stage. Only three have speaking roles but the playwright tells us in his introduction that all the characters are on stage all the time, "progressing and enhancing the action whenever possible." What roles could you imagine for these other actors? Lanier's family in his past? His mother or wife? Vonzia? How would Vonzia respond, seeing her father in this moment from his past? As an actor, how will this moment watching your father inform and strengthen your work in your own scene? You may want to read the whole play to find out more about these characters and ghosts from Lanier's past.

PLAYWRIGHT AND PRODUCTIONS

Robert Chafe lives in St. John's, Newfoundland, and is Artistic Director of Artistic Fraud Newfoundland, a theatre company he co-founded with theatre director Jillian Keiley. Artistic Fraud developed and produced the first production of *Oil and Water* in 2011 before touring the play to Toronto and other cities across Canada.

READING AND RESEARCHING

Related Resources

Below is a list of websites and online resources covering various aspects of the civil rights movement:

www.civilrights.org/resources/civilrights101/desegregation.html

www.africanamericanart.si.edu

www.facinghistory.org/for-educators/educator-resources/
lessons-and-units/pivotal-moment-civil-rights-movement

www.crmvet.org

Robert Chafe and *Oil and Water*:

www.playwrightsguild.ca/playwright/robert-chafe

www.charpo-canada.com/2012/04/sunday-read-robert-chafe-on-oil-and.html

Related Plays and Readings

Skin by Dennis Foon

The Real McCoy by Andrew Moodie

Toronto the Good by Andrew Moodie

Beatdown: Three Plays by Joseph Jomo Pierre

Afrika, Solo by Djanet Sears

Give Voice: Ten Twenty-Minute Plays from the Obsidian Theatre Company edited by Rita Shelton Deverell

No Great Mischief by Alistair MacLeod

The Breakwater Book of Contemporary Newfoundland Plays, volumes 1 and 2, edited by Denyse Lynde

NORAH'S ARK
BY JASMINE DUBÉ, TRANSLATED BY LINDA GABORIAU

THE PLAY

Norah is the sole survivor of a fatal flood. She finds herself alone, on a little boat, in the middle of a menacing ocean. She has had to leave quickly and so has only been able to bring a few practical and special items with her. As she navigates her way between hope and despair, she creates a new world for herself using three treasures: her knowledge, her memories, and her imagination.

THE MONOLOGUE

In this scene, Norah has survived a storm and is hungry. The dialogue in italics are either Norah's inner voice or her mother's voice. These lines can be spoken by the actor or be pre-recorded. The English translation appears first here, followed by the monologue in the original French.

THE CHARACTER

Norah: A child who has survived a flood. She is alone on a makeshift boat in the middle of the ocean.

MONOLOGUE

English: Norah's Ark

NORAH *takes out a photo album. She speaks to the photos in the album.*

NORAH: Hi, Grandma. You're still standing there beside your old car. You're cold? For sure. *(like a reproach to the sky)* It's freezing here. Come, we'll keep each other warm.

She presses the photo to her heart. She turns a page in the album.

What did you say, Mum? Of course, I'm making sure I eat properly.

She takes a strand of spaghetti and carefully breaks it into portions, then eats it.

Mmmmm. That's good. I love it when you cook shepherd's pie and hot soup with vegetables and rice. Oooof . . . I'm not hungry anymore.

Beat.

Dessert? You know I can't resist your chocolate cake.

She eats a tiny bit of cookie.

Mmmmm. This is the best cake you ever made.

She gives a crumb to her bird.

Even my bird agrees. He's cooing his heart out, it's so good.

She puts some crumbs between the pages of the photo album.

And my goldfish, too. And my cat.

She looks at the picture of her father.

All right, Daddy, I'll clean up my room.

She sweeps with a pine bough, singing as she cleans.

Row row row your boat
Gently down the stream
Merrily merrily merrily merrily
Life is but a dream . . .

You're the one who taught me that song, Daddy. I'd never rowed a boat before . . . I had to learn. I left a long time ago. I can't remember when. Was it a week ago? Or a month or a year or eighteen thousand days?

Our house doesn't exist anymore. The roof collapsed. "We'll find each other. Don't be scared, sweetie." *We'll find each other. Don't be scared, sweetie.* That's what my mother said before she disappeared on the strangest boat in the world. My cat was with her. *They say cats have nine lives.*

I'm going to tell you what I brought with me, okay? First of all, my bird. My *Little Prince* book. A book of matches. A notebook and a pencil. An address book, hmmpff! A can of sardines. I ate them two days ago, but I kept the can. A bag of cookies. I'm trying to make them last. A package of spaghetti. Your coat, Dad. A bottle of juice. Some water. A candle. A bottle of whiskey. A pack of Kleenex. But they're all wet 'cause I dropped them in the water. There are eighty-six spaghettis left in the box.

She nibbles on one.

Eighty-five and three quarters.

She nibbles some more.

Eighty-five and a half. Right. Now there are eighty-five and a half spaghettis left.

A can of tomato juice. I hate tom . . . my mum must've put that in the trunk.

Beat.

But I'll drink it at the very, very, very end, if I'm really, really, really thirsty and I really, really can't stand it anymore, more, more, more. When it reaches that point, they say tomato juice is better than . . . than nothing at all.

Mum told me: "*Take what's most important to you. We'll bring some bare essentials, just in case . . . but I don't think we'll need to use them. Don't worry, little mouse.*"

Beat. She finds a little box.

Mum brought the box you keep your secrets in, Daddy.

She opens it.

It's full of papers. A birth certificate. What's a mortgage, Dad? Mortgage, baggage . . . A will and testament . . . is that when you die? "We leave everything to our daughter, Norah: the house at 843 Shore Road." There's nothing left. It's not worth a thing now. No more roof. No more walls. No more swings. No more Shore Road. No more shore. Just water. Salty water.

(She reads an envelope.) "To be given to Norah, after my death."

Beat.

Do your own errands. I'm not your survivant.

She puts the letter away angrily.

Electricity bill: $46.84. I won't pay it. There's no heat here, and the service is bad. *(speaking to the sky)* You hear me? The service is bad.

She burns the electricity bill.

At least I'll put it to some use.

I've finished cleaning up, Daddy. This is all I own. I have a houseboat. I have papers. Fish, you're the ministers. We are the government. And the government resigns. I declare Jonah the new president of life.

She opens the album to the page with Jonah's photograph.

Mum, why didn't you want me to bring Jonah?

"Don't be silly. You can't take a goldfish in your suitcase, Norah. It's impossible."

Norah looks at the picture of her goldfish.

Jonah was my friend. He knew how to keep a secret. He glowed like a sun in the water.

Light. Wind. The sea is rough. NORAH is holding on to her boat for dear life.

If I arrive ashore, somewhere, I promise I'll . . . I promise anything you want.

Blackout.

Français: L'arche de Noémie

NOÉMIE sort un album à photos. Elle s'adresse aux photos de l'album.

NOÉMIE: Salut grand-maman; tu es encore devant ta vieille auto. Tu as froid? C'est sûr. *(comme un reproche au ciel)* On gèle ici. Viens, on va se réchauffer.

Elle serre la photo sur son coeur. Elle tourne une page de l'album.

Qu'est-ce que tu dis, maman? Bien sûr, que j'oublie pas de bien manger.

Elle prend un spaghetti qu'elle coupe minutieusement en portions et qu'elle mange.

Hum! C'est bon. J'adore ça quand tu fais du pâté chinois et de la soupe chaude avec des légumes et du riz. Ouf . . . J'ai plus faim.

Temps.

Du dessert? Tu sais bien que je peux pas résister à ton gâteau au chocolat.

Elle mange un bout de biscuit.

Mmmm. C'est le meilleur que tu as jamais fait.

Elle en donne une miette à l'oiseau.

Même mon oiseau est d'accord. Il se roucoule par terre tellement c'est bon.

Elle met des miettes entre les pages de l'album à photos.

Et mon poisson rouge aussi. Et mon chat.

Elle regarde la photo de son père.

Bon d'accord, papa je vais faire mon ménage.

Elle balaie avec une cime de pin en chantonnant:

Il était un petit navire, il était un petit navire
qui n'avait ja-ja-jamais navigué
qui n'avait ja-ja-jamais navigué. Ohé . . . Ohé . . .

C'est toi qui m'as appris cette chanson-là, papa. Je n'avais jamais navigué avant . . . Il a fallu que j'apprenne. Ça fait longtemps que je suis partie. Je me souviens plus c'était quand. C'était il y a 16 jours? ou un mois ou un an ou dix huit mille jours?

Notre maison n'existe plus. Son toit s'est cassé. «Nous nous retrouverons. N'aie pas peur, ma chérie.» *Nous nous retrouverons. N'aie pas peur, ma chérie.* C'est ça qu'elle a dit, ma mère avant de disparaître sur le plus étrange bateau du monde. Mon chat était avec elle. *On dit que les chats ont sept vies.*

Je vais te dire ce qu'on a apporté, o.k.? Premièrement, mon oiseau. Le livre du petit Prince. Un carton d'allumettes. Un cahier, un crayon. Un carnet d'adresse Pfff . . . Une boîte de sardines. Je l'ai mangée il y a deux jours mais j'ai gardé la boîte. Un sac de biscuits; je les ménage. Une boîte de spaghettis. Ton manteau, papa. Une bouteille de jus. De l'eau. Une bougie. Une bouteille de vin. Un paquet de kleenex. Mais ils sont tout mouillés parce que je les ai échappés dans l'eau. Il reste 86 spaghettis dans la boîte.

   Elle en grignote un.

85 et 3/4.

   Elle grignote encore.

85 et demi. C'est ça. Il reste 85 spaghettis et demi.

Une canne de jus de tomate, j'haïs le j . . . c'est maman qui a mis ça dans le coffre.

   Temps.

Mais je le boirai à la toute toute toute toute fin, si j'ai vraiment vraiment vraiment soif et que j'en peux vraiment vraiment vraiment pu pu pu. Dans ce temps-là il paraît qu'il vaut mieux du jus de tomate que . . . que rien du tout.

Maman m'a dit: «*Ramasse ce qui est le plus important pour toi. Nous prendrons des choses de première nécessité, au cas où . . . mais je ne crois pas que nous aurons à nous en servir. Sois sans crainte, ma puce.*»

Temps. Elle trouve un coffret.

Maman a apporté votre coffre à secrets, papa.

Elle l'ouvre.

C'est plein de papiers. Certificat de naissance. C'est quoi une hypothèque, papa? Hypothèque, roulathèque . . . Un testament, c'est quand on meurt? «Nous léguons tout à notre fille Noémie: la maison au 843 Chemin du Bord de l'eau.» Il y a pu rien. Ça vaut plus rien. Plus de toit. Plus de mur. Plus de balançoire. Même plus de chemin du Bord de l'eau. Même plus de bord de l'eau. Juste de l'eau. Salée.

(Elle lit sur une enveloppe.) «A remettre à Noémie après ma mort.»

Temps.

Tu feras tes commissions toi-même. Je suis pas votre servivante.

Elle range la lettre, rageusement.

Compte d'électricité 46,84$. Je le payerai pas. Il y a pas de chauffage ici, et le service est mauvais.

(elle s'adresse au ciel) Vous entendez? Le service est mauvais.

Elle brûle le compte d'électricité.

Ça va au moins servir à quelque chose.

J'ai fini le ménage, papa. C'est tout ce que je possède. J'ai une maison bateau. J'ai des papiers. Poissons vous êtes ministres. Ici c'est le gouvernement. Le gouvernement démissionne. Et c'est Jonas le nouveau président de la vie.

Elle ouvre l'album à la page où se trouve la photo de Jonas.

Maman, pourquoi tu as pas voulu que j'apporte Jonas?

«On ne peut pas apporter un poisson rouge au fond d'une valise, voyons. C'est impossible, Noémie.»

NOÉMIE regarde la photo de son poisson.

Jonas, c'était mon ami. Il savait garder un secret, lui. Il était comme un soleil dans l'eau

Lumière. Il vente. La mer est agitée. Noémie se cramponne à sa barque.

Si j'arrive sur une terre, quelque part, je promets que . . . je promets tout ce que vous voudrez.

Noir.

NOTES TO THE ACTORS AND DIRECTORS

How old is Norah? The playwright describes her as a child, which is vague but allows you to find the child you are most comfortable playing. Will you be six? Eight? Ten? You will want to connect with the child inside of you but also, as research, play with a real child to remind and inspire you. Pretend you're alone on the ocean in a boat. Make it a game.

Whether you perform the lines in italics yourself or pre-record them, you will want to choose another voice and physicality for these characters.

For further strategies to explore and rehearse the monologue, turn to the Monologue Map on page 179.

PLAYWRIGHT AND PRODUCTIONS

Jasmine Dubé is an accomplished actor, playwright, director, and author from Quebec. *Norah's Ark* was written in French as *L'arche de Noémie*, and was nominated for a Governor General's Literary Award in 2000 for French Drama. The French-language premiere took place at Théâtre Bouches Décousues in 1998. It was translated by Linda Gaboriau one of Canada's foremost literary translators.

A BOMB IN THE HEART
BY WAJDI MOUAWAD, TRANSLATED BY LINDA GABORIAU

THE PLAY

A sudden phone call sends nineteen-year-old Wahab out into the night to be by his dying mother in a hospital. As he fights through a blistering snowstorm his real struggles are those in his mind. How did he get here? What does he feel? Who has he become?

THE MONOLOGUE

We all tell stories about our lives, but how do we decide when that story begins? How do we even know it's begun? This is the reflection that begins Wajdi Mouawad's *A Bomb in the Heart*. But is this the calm reflection of old age? The central character is not old—he (though this scene could be played by a woman) is only nineteen. From the title we gather there is "a bomb in the heart." Is it his heart?

THE CHARACTER

Wahab: Nineteen years old.

MONOLOGUE

English: *A Bomb in the Heart*

WAHAB: You never know how a story begins. I mean, when a story begins and it reaches you, you don't know, when that story first begins, that it's beginning. I mean . . . it's not like, there you are, quietly walking down the street and suddenly you say to yourself: hey, this is the beginning of a story. I mean, you don't realize it . . . Then, when you finally realize that you're in the middle of a story, you don't know how it will end. No one can know. Until it's over. Until it's run its course and you open your eyes and say: the story is over. It's over and because it's over, you start to hear the silence, the deep silence that almost drowned you. Totally. So, to ward off silence, you try to find the words. To tell the story. A word that surfaces deep inside you, any word, is like an oasis in the middle of the desert. You pounce on it and drink it. You drink the word.

The first word I found to tell this story was the word "before." But saying "before" is new to me. Sometimes I say, "I was just a kid, before." When did I stop? I don't know. That's just how it is now. I hear old people talking. They say: "Before the war." That is a definite before. The war is definite. Or: "Before the death of so and so." That's definite too. Death is definite. Before. I don't know.

My name is Abdelwahab, like the singer, but everyone calls me Wahab. I am nineteen and recently I've been able to say "before," and sometimes it's a catastrophe.

How did it all begin . . . I don't know.

I can't say I heard the phone ring. I can't say that. I can only say that I was sitting on my bed wondering if I'd dreamt it. That was possible. It was nighttime, it was cold. Was I dreaming? Then I heard it ring, like an answer: "You weren't dreaming." But I could have been. Outside, there was a storm and the snow-removal equipment was making a racket. A real uproar. It could have been a dream. But I found myself holding the receiver in my hand. I said hello in a normal voice. Someone said: "Wahab?" I said, yes. Someone said: "Get here fast."

Français: Un obus dans le coeur

WAHAB: On ne sait jamais comment une histoire commence. Je veux dire que lorsqu'une histoire commence et que cette histoire vous arrive à vous, vous ne savez pas, au moment où elle commence, qu'elle commence. Je veux dire, on ne le sait pas comment tout ça va se terminer. Personne ne peut savoir. C'est seulement à la fin. Lorsque tout est consommé, qu'on ouvre les yeux et qu'on se dit: l'histoire est terminée. Elle est terminée et parce qu'elle est terminée, vous vous mettez à entendre le silence, le grand silence qui a failli vous noyer. C'est comme ça. Alors, pour conjurer le silence, on tente de trouver les mots. Pour raconter. Même si c'est n'importe quoi, mais un mot qu'on trouve au fond de soi, c'est comme une oasis au milieu du désert. On se précipite dessus et on le boit. On boit le mot.

Moi, le premier mot que j'ai trouvé pour pouvoirraconter ce qui s'est passé, c'est le mot «avant.» Je dis «avant,» mais cela ne fait pas longtemps que je peux dire «avant.» Je dis parfois: «Avant, j'étais un enfant.» Mais quand est-ce que j'ai cessé? Je ne sais pas. C'est comme ça maintenant. J'entends les vieux qui parlent. Ils disent: «Avant la guerre.» C'est un avant fixe. La guerre c'est fixe. Parfois aussi: «Avant la mort d'un tel.» Ça aussi c'est fixe. La mort est fixe. Avant. Je ne sais pas.

Je m'appelle Abdelwahab, comme le chanteur, mais tout le monde m'appelle Wahab, j'ai dix-neuf ans et depuis peu, je peux dire le mot "avant" et c'est parfois une catasrophe.

Comment tout ça a commencé . . . Je ne sais pas.

Je ne peux pas dire que je l'ai entendu sonner. Je ne peux pas dire. Je peux juste dire que je me suis retrouvé assis dans mon lit à me demander si j'avais rêvé. C'était possible. Il faisait nuit, il faisait froid. Est-ca que j'ai rêvé? Puis je l'ai enentdu sonner comme une réponse: «Tu n'as pas rêvé.» Mais ça aurait pu. Dehors c'était la tempête et toutes les machines de déneigement qui faisaient leur raffut. Un vrai boucan. J'aurais pu rêver. Pourtant je me suis retrouvé le combiné à la main. J'ai dit allô d'une voix normale. On a dit: «Wahab?» J'ai dit oui. On m'a dit: «Viens vite.»

NOTES TO THE ACTORS AND DIRECTORS

The text has an urgency that is reminiscent of *The Middle Place*. Short, punchy sentences contrasted by pauses (indicated by the ellipses). But unlike *The Middle Place*, the language here isn't natural; it is heightened, dramatic, even poetic. The playwright uses strong words: death, desert, catastrophe. The monologue needs to be spoken with clarity so warm up your voice and practise a few articulation exercises before beginning.

For further strategies to explore and rehearse the monologue, turn to the Monologue Map on page 179.

PLAYWRIGHT AND PRODUCTIONS

Wajdi Mouawad was born in Lebanon in 1968 and grew up in Beirut and Paris before immigrating to Canada and settling in Montreal. His play *Incendies* was adapted into the Oscar-nominated film of the same name. *Un obus dans le coeur* was originally produced by Théâtre de Sartrouville-CDN in Sartrouville, France, in 2005. The English-language premiere of *A Bomb in the Heart* was presented in February 2014 by Downstage in Calgary, in a translation by Linda Gaboriau.

PERFORMANCE POSSIBILITIES

There are a variety of ways to share and present your work. We have suggested one possibility with each scene, but below are examples that you may wish to try instead of the suggestions. Some will work better with certain monologues or scenes than others. Discuss with your partner or group which presentation strategy works best for your chosen piece, or come up with your own strategies for presenting your scene using these examples as maps. Following your presentation, discuss and deconstruct the performed scene or monologue as a class, within a group, or with your partner.

Divide the scene into two or three sections and have one group present the first part, the second group present the middle part, and the third group present the final part. Try to move from group to group seamlessly using the same props and set.

Share your understanding of the essence of the scene by choosing a snippet of three or four consecutive lines. Bookend this essence with two still images/tableaux from the scene to further represent the meaning.

Select four or five key consecutive lines from the scene and distill each line into one word that exemplifies the meaning of the line. For example, "I wish I hadn't done that!" could be distilled into the word "sorry." Share your scene or monologue using only these distilled words.

Share your the scene using only gestures.

Present two selections from the scene and use a narrator to fill in between lines (an aside to the audience, a statement of feelings, etc.).

Use different formations to help present. You can create a straight line with your backs to audience, and then turn to the front to say your line and then return to the first position when finished.

Improvise and present a section of the scene or monologue in your own words.

Improvise and present the scene that happens before the provided scene or monologue.

Select and organize five to ten lines from the scene or monologue into a choral-speaking presentation.

Choose two or three snippets and decide on a different order to present the selections instead of chronologically.

Work with a partner and deliver the subtext of each line of the scene or monologue.

Work with a partner or group and create the soundscape behind the scene.

Perform and present the scene or monologue as it is written in the traditional manner.

MONOLOGUE MAP

As you explore your monologue, use these strategies to unpack the text, make meaning, and uncover truths about the character and this moment they are sharing with you. These strategies will help you to gain a deeper understanding of this character to bring a rich and multi-layered portrayal to the audience.

Connecting With the Monologue

Notes on Connecting With the Monologue

Students may want to research the context of the monologue to better understand the character at some point in the exploration process. To begin the opening up or unpacking process, students should read through the monologue several times, answering some key questions through their first impressions.

Monologues may be chosen for independent work while others are working on group scenes, or have all students work on monologues at the same time.

Read the monologue silently to yourself several times to meet the character. Consider first impressions:

Who is speaking?

Who might they be speaking to?

What is their story about?

How similar or dissimilar is this character to you?

Who do they remind you of in your own life?

Exploring Meaning

Text Play

Read the monologue out loud. Do not think about emotions and gestures at this point, you are simply reading and hearing the words.

Read aloud while walking through the room, changing your pace as you read.

Select a focus in the room and read aloud concentrating on that spot.

Read aloud with the same focus but this time read the monologue as though it was an important speech you were delivering at the UN, as though it was a gossip piece, as though it was a set of instructions, or as though it was the most exciting moment in your life and you wanted everyone to know about it.

Move through the room reading with a sense of urgency and then try reading it again completely relaxed.

Move through the space while reading, changing tempo, pace, and volume.

Read the monologue walking slowly through the space. As you are walking transform into the character physically, considering how the character would stand, and then move slowly into the role and then back to yourself. Repeat the process.

Consider how the character would hold their shoulders and carry tension as you continue reading.

Read the entire monologue as though you are angry, sad, afraid, happy, and excited.

Consider when the movement or vocal changes felt truthful or authentic.

Share with a partner your thoughts about the character at this point.

Questions

What five things do you know for sure about the character from their words?

What are five unanswered questions about the character or monologue?

Is there anything you wonder about?

Think of five questions you would want to ask the character.

Notes on Text Play

Encourage the students to discover the character through the activities, and not to make assumptions and decisions yet.

Choose a variety of ways to unpack the words and ideas in the monologue. Look to some of the scene exercises for further examples that would be appropriate for unpacking monologues.

Giving the students new ways to read the text will also assist in memorizing the piece.

Where is the character when they are delivering this monologue? What were they doing before speaking?

How do you feel about the character? Why is their story important to share?

How would you want an audience to feel about the character?

Document your questions, rereading the monologue if needed.

Share with a partner, a group, or the whole class, noting similarities and differences between the questions.

Building Authentic Characters and Relationships

Listening

Work with a partner and read your monologue aloud to them.

Invite your partner to read your monologue out loud to you while you listen with your eyes closed.

Repeat the activity with the partner's monologue.

Discuss what you learned about the monologues and the characters through listening.

Listening in Role

Work with a partner and choose a role for them to play while listening to you read your monologue. The role should be someone who is close to your character, their mother, a friend, a spouse, etc.

Read the monologue, remembering who they are in the character's life and responding to them authentically.

Notes on Writing in Role

This writing activity could be shared with the partners or with the class. The writing could be integrated before or after the monologue to create a dialogue.

Questioning in Role

In their given role, have the listener ask the reader thoughtful questions to help them further understand the monologue.

Repeat the activity with your partner reading their monologue.

Writing in Role

In role as the listening character you assigned to your partner, write a brief monologue in response to what you just heard.

Notes on Costumes and Props

Being in costume can often assist in bringing the character's body movements and mannerisms to life. Encourage students to rehearse the monologue while dressed in partial costume and to consider and then select personal and/or set artifacts to further encourage character behaviours and circumstances.

Bring in some artifacts for students to choose from, but they may also bring in their own as needed.

Costumes and Props

Carefully consider costumes and props to further develop your character and performance. Bring in objects from home to add to any that may already be available. It is important not to make up your mind beforehand, but to bring in a range of possibilities.

Consider socio-economic background, personality, time period, and context when choosing costumes and props.

As you work through the monologue, try different possibilities until you are satisfied that you have chosen the items that best suit your character's personality and circumstances.

Create a Working Set

Notes on Creating a Working Set

Defining the working space for students who are exploring monologues will assist them in preparing their pieces, and in building belief.

Define the area that will be your working set and choose where you will place personal props or props for the set.

Use chairs to represent items such as furniture or items of fabric to create a sense of outside space or a change of location.

Use anything at hand that will help you to build belief in the environment (set).

Rehearsing/Presenting

Go to page 177. There are a variety of ways to present the monologue, and to discuss and deconstruct the presentations.

Reflecting

Beyond First Impressions

What do you now know about your character that you weren't aware of when first reading the monologue?

Beyond First Impressions Notes

Encourage the students to reflect on how they learned about the character and moved to deeper understandings from their first impressions.

How do you feel about your character? If you could speak to this person, what would you want to tell them? Would you offer support or advice?

What have you learned about your character that surprised you?

In what ways is this character similar or not similar to yourself?

Select one important strategy that changed your work and interpretation of your character. Reflect on why this strategy was so effective. Would you use the same strategy again to understand other characters?

How difficult was it to work on your own with your monologue?

Snippet Sharing

If you could choose only three lines to tell the story of the monologue, what three lines would you choose? On your own choose a snippet that represents the essence of the monologue.

Practise saying your snippet to best communicate the main idea of the piece.

Create a gesture or movement for the snippet.

Working in a group of three, move around the circle presenting your snippets of text with movement and gesture.

Negotiate how you might weave and sequence each piece together into a new mini text.

Begin with a group tableau and end with a group tableau. Give this piece a title.

Share with another group or class.

Return to your monologue and incorporate this new learning.

Character Memoir

With a partner, imagine you are going to write the memoir of your character and brainstorm a list of areas to consider focusing on.

Using this list, individually create an imagined life story for your character. As much as possible support your ideas with hints from the text.

Share your memoir with another pair of students or with a small group and elicit feedback on your choices to ensure authenticity.

Write a list of chapters from the memoir. If there is a copy of the full play available, compare your list with the information in the scenes.

Character Memoir Notes

Create a list for students to help then with their memoir. Ask them to consider:

- family situation

- relationships

- age

- health

- beliefs/ambitions

- attitude towards life (rebellious, serious, optimistic, resentful, sense of humour, etc.)

- occupation/work

- social class

- level of education, school (worst and best subjects)

- type of home, neighbourhood

- anything else that might effect or have affected the character

GLOSSARY OF DRAMA STRATEGIES

Drama strategies and conventions are practices and forms of representation that are widely accepted for use in drama instruction. They have been expanded upon, added to, and further developed by many practitioners. An instructor will select a strategy to assist the students to make personal connections to the work, to make meaning of the situation, and scaffold the learning to deepen understanding.

Carousel

The carousel is a strategy for sharing and or presenting scenes. Students prepare a short scene or image and bring the work to a group circle. The work is shared seamlessly with one group after the other, presenting and then freezing until each group has shared. Discussion follows the carousel.

Choral Speaking

Students read aloud written texts, assigning parts among group members. The text may be divided into individual, small group, and whole group parts and then presented or shared together. In preparing a choral-speaking piece students will experiment with voice, sound, gesture, and movement.

Collective Role

More than one person simultaneously assumes one role. Any one of the students can speak as the character that is being portrayed. Working collectively provides students with a variety of interpretations to enhance their portrayal of the character.

Corridor of Voices

The class forms two facing lines, creating an alley, and at a crucial moment in a character's life when an issue must be resolved, the character walks through this alley. Students on either side may represent people in the character's life and offer support, advice, warnings, or judgments. As the character reaches the end of the corridor he or she may decide what course of action to take.

A Day in the Life

Students explore the experience of a character by working backwards from a significant moment or turning point in that person's life to build the story that accounts for the event.

Students work in groups using tableau, improvisation, and/or role-play to depict key moments that may have occurred within a twenty-four-hour period of the character's life. The scenes are then run in chronological order to depict the events leading up to the dramatically significant moment.

Defining Space

Students, negotiating together, use available materials and furniture to define and create a key space in the scene. The selection and placement of objects, props, and furniture is decided and justified by the students. This activity can lead to a discussion of set and design.

Flashback and Flash Forward

This strategy is used to deepen the understanding of a character by creating the backstory and/or imaging the character's future. Scenes can be explored from an earlier point of time (flashback) to explain the causes of an action in the present. Students can also show an action in a later time by considering its imagined or actual outcome (flash forward).

Hot Seat

A student takes on a role and is interviewed or questioned by a partner or by the rest of the group. The questioners may speak as themselves or in role. A chair is usually designated as the hot seat, a place for characters to sit and receive questions.

If I Were You

Students approach a character in a key moment in the scene or at the end of the scene and place their hands on the character's shoulder and complete the sentence, "If I were you . . . " This strategy will encourage empathy and reflection.

Instructor in Role

When an instructor works in role, she or he adopts a set of attitudes to work with the students. Acting skill is not required, but when an instructor chooses to take on a role, he or she must alter his or her status in the classroom to help students explore issues or examine possible directions that a drama may take. When the instructor works in role she or he models thoughtful, authentic role-play to give the students a sense of what they should be striving for in their own role-play and portrayal of characters.

Memory Circle

In reflecting on a scene or a situation in a scene following the presentation, students form a circle and in role share a memory of the moment in their lives that was depicted in the scene. They might use a line from the scene in their memory. For example, "I remember feeling . . . " "I remember saying . . . "

Objects of Character

Props, posters, maps, letters, or media materials are used to establish a character, depict a setting, and/or advance a story. Objects of character begin the discussion and selection of props in a play.

Overheard Conversations

Students role-play in small groups, listening in (eavesdropping) on what is being said by different characters in the drama. For this convention, a signal is often given to freeze all the groups, who then in turn are each "brought to life" to continue improvising while the other groups, as the audience, watch and listen. The instructor can also pass by as if she/he is someone eavesdropping on each scene.

Questioning

Questions are used by the instructor (and students) both inside and outside drama explorations, both in role and out of role, to give purpose, direction, and shape to the learning activities. Questions can deepen belief and commitment and can stimulate the minds of the students to go beyond what they already know.

Role On the Wall

A central role to be explored in the scene is represented in picture form, as a diagram or outline on a chart, which is then put on the wall. Students reflect on the thoughts, feelings, and qualities that are significant to the character by adding words or statements or questions to the page. Information about the role is added as the characters and scene is introduced and progresses.

Soundscape

Sounds are used to create an atmosphere or to enhance the important moments of a scene. Students usually work in groups to agree on and produce the desired sound effects using voice and/or instruments.

The Space Between

Students place themselves in a physical position to depict their relationship to each other at a moment in the scene. This will encourage them to ask important questions about their characters, such as, What changes might occur over time? What name might be given to identify this space between the two characters? How will we alter this space?

Tableau/Still Image

Working alone, with a partner, or in small groups, students become motionless figures to represent a scene, theme, important moment(s) in a narrative, or an abstract idea.

Important features of a tableau include character, space, gesture, facial expression, and levels. Still images can be shared by one group watching another, or the class can be an audience as the work is presented.

Thought Tracking

This convention is used to find out what characters are thinking at a particular moment in the scene. Thought tracking makes public the in-role thoughts, questions, or feelings of a character or characters. Most commonly, a signal such as a tap on the shoulder is given for the character to speak a thought out loud or to complete a prompt such as, "I am feeling . . . " or "I am thinking . . . " Innermost thoughts can also be shared as the instructor passes by. This strategy will encourage students to think about motivation and subtext in a scene.

Writing in Role

Students write from the point of view of a character either mentioned within or active in a scene to reflect on the situation and deepen understanding of the character. Some examples of forms include diaries, journals, letters, and reports that can also be shaped into monologues.

ACKNOWLEDGEMENTS

Thanks to Larry Swartz for collaborating and sharing with us in the creation of the *Kim's Convenience* teaching and learning strategies.

Debbie Nyman is an instructor of the Dramatic Arts Additional Qualifications program at the Ontario Institute of Studies in Education at the University of Toronto. She was a classroom dramatic arts teacher and instructional leader with the Toronto District School Board for several years. Debbie has authored documents and resources at the board and ministry levels and is the co-author of *Drama Schemes, Themes and Dreams* (Pembroke Publishers).

Jill Lloyd-Jones has been a drama teacher and instructional leader for many years at the Toronto District School Board. She has worked collaboratively with all levels of educators in Ontario to support innovation in the teaching of dramatic arts and movement. She was also a writer of the two popular TDSB Treasures for Teaching documents. Having just moved to the UK, Jill is working as a freelance consultant, tells people she really is not American, and is getting used to the rain.

David S. Craig is one of Canada's most prolific and successful dramatists. He has written twenty-nine professionally produced dramatic works, including his hit comedy *Having Hope at Home* and the internationally acclaimed *Danny, King of the Basement*. Other successful plays include *Smokescreen*, which has been translated into five languages, his award-winning adaptation of Carlo Goldoni's *The Fan*, and his adaptation of Michel Ende's *The Neverending Story*. He is the co-founder of two professional theatres for young audiences–Theatre Direct and Roseneath Theatre. In 2014, the City of Toronto awarded Mr. Craig the Barbara Hamilton Memorial Award for excellence in the performing arts.

First edition: October 2014
Printed and bound in Canada by Marquis Book Printing, Montreal

Cover design by Christine Mangosing // CMango Design

PLAYWRIGHTS
CANADA PRESS

202-269 Richmond Street West
Toronto, ON
M5V 1X1

416.703.0013
info@playwrightscanada.com
playwrightscanada.com